# AGENCY
## at
# WORK

The Secret to Going from
Burnt Out to Fired Up
in the Modern Workplace

# AGENCY
## at
# WORK

The Secret to Going from
Burnt Out to Fired Up
in the Modern Workplace

## Indro Roy

**World Scientific**

NEW JERSEY • LONDON • SINGAPORE • BEIJING • SHANGHAI • TAIPEI • CHENNAI

*Published by*

World Scientific Publishing Co. Pte. Ltd.
5 Toh Tuck Link, Singapore 596224
*USA office:* 27 Warren Street, Suite 401-402, Hackensack, NJ 07601
*UK office:* 57 Shelton Street, Covent Garden, London WC2H 9HE

Library of Congress Control Number: 2025027023

**British Library Cataloguing-in-Publication Data**
A catalogue record for this book is available from the British Library.

**AGENCY AT WORK**
**The Secret to Going from Burnt Out to Fired Up in the Modern Workplace**

ISBN 978-981-98-1587-6 (hardcover)
ISBN 978-981-98-1665-1 (paperback)
ISBN 978-981-98-1588-3 (ebook for institutions)
ISBN 978-981-98-1589-0 (ebook for individuals)

For any available supplementary material, please visit
https://www.worldscientific.com/worldscibooks/10.1142/14384#t=suppl

Desk Editor: Geysilla Jean Ortiz
Cover Design: Lionel Seow

Project Managed and Typeset by Manila Typesetting Company (MTC)

# About the Author

I ndro Roy is an Executive Director at Deloitte in South East Asia.

Based out of Singapore, Indro is a member of the Executive Team, leads the CEO Program, and is the leader for Human Capital Advisory practice of the firm.

His experience spans almost 3 decades of consulting, starting with Hewitt Associates, where he managed their SE Asia practices, and built the global Leadership Consulting practice across 17 countries.

He then transitioned to Korn Ferry, building the leadership and talent consulting practices across Asia Pacific. In this role, he helped shape the consulting proposition and built a team of professionals across Australia, India, SE Asia, Greater China, Japan and Korea.

In 2016, Indro transitioned to Deloitte to shape the global leadership consulting practice and was then asked to lead the global Future of Work Center of Excellence, located in Singapore, in partnership with the government. The thought leadership and proposition that was built in this centre evolved into the Workforce Transformation practice that he then led for the SE Asian markets.

Indro has a dual background in technology and psychology. This has, over time, helped him understand the impact that new technologies and innovation have on work, workforce, and workplace. His work with senior leadership teams and boards further informs his thought leadership on governance and culture in the organization.

His clients range from governments to large multinational organizations mostly in financial services, technology, and consumer businesses. His work covers a wide array of organization, leadership and talent topics, but his personal obsession has been in creating organization cultures that foster innovation, speed and collective success. This focus led him to undertake deep research on the question"How can we prepare modern workforces to thrive in extreme uncertainty?".

Indro's new book, *Agency at Work: The Secret to Going from Burnt Out to Fired Up in the Modern Workplace,* brings together his research findings on this topic and his personal experience helping clients thrive in chaos.

# Contents

# Preface

The industrial revolution made our muscles redundant. Today, we view our muscles more through the lens of aesthetics than in the context of work. The AI revolution, in particular, the emerging adoption of agentic AI, is rapidly doing the same to our technical knowledge and professional ability. What we will be left with, therefore, is our own human agency.

Human agency is our ability to be self-motivated, self-driven, and self-correcting, in applying our unique human ability to spot and solve everyday problems.

I believe that in parallel with our global efforts to develop and deploy agentic AI (machine agency), we must unlock human agency in ourselves, our teams, and our organizations. This combination will create a period of incredible innovation, growth, and success around us. We will no longer feel anxious about our work, jobs, and careers. We will finally learn to thrive at work.

This belief drew me to my research on agency. I looked for individuals who are perceived to operate with a high level of agency by their peers.

In the process of identifying these individuals, their peers shared the following observations.

They ...

"... are always calm and focused, not flustered by the chaos around us."

"... seem to have time, are never rushed, always open to meet up and discuss things of value."

"... are quietly confident, always comfortable to try and make something happen."

"... are infinitely resourceful—within their wide network, they will find a friend who can help."

"... are learning and growing constantly—even without formal training and development."

"... seek out feedback—never defensive, always keen to know what can be better next time."

Over the last 4 years, I interviewed them one by one to find what makes them different.

What I found is extremely encouraging for all of us.

Human agency is not a DNA trait but a skill that can be developed and built. The best part is that it can be built at any organizational level and context. You don't need to be a senior executive to develop a sense of agency. All you need is the discipline to practice a set of habits every day.

It shows up in three zones:

1. Personal agency, or the feeling that you have the steering wheel in your hands at all times.
2. Social agency, or the feeling that your network of relationships always has someone who can help.
3. Growth agency, or the feeling that you are learning and growing objectively every day.

These zones have specific rules or habits that can be understood and applied straight away—just 10 rules in all.

Finally, the best part of human agency is that it can be measured with seven simple questions.

In other words, what I found is that the few individuals who exhibit high agency around us today carry with them a practical and specific set of 'instructions' that we can all learn and leverage in our work every day. This is the key to our ability to thrive in a world of extreme uncertainty and succeed in the context of agentic AI and machine intelligence.

Having applied this playbook to myself, my own team, and several client organizations, I have come to a simple conclusion.

Organizations with high agency leaders and high agency teams are not only going to outperform their competition, they will pull away from the rest of the pack with pace. They will be faster to market with new propositions, significantly more efficient with resources, seamless and calm in adapting to changes in the environment, and operating with a culture of thriving in uncertainty.

This journey is not only actionable but also observable and measurable. Business and human capital leaders can come together and work on this journey that benefits both the business outcomes and the mental health of employees, at the same time.

My hope for the future of work is that, as AI grows and takes over so much of what we consider human work today, we unlock our own agency to flourish alongside these advancements. Let *Agency at Work* be your playbook, guiding you professionally and personally, and helping you thrive throughout your journey.

Indro
2025

# PART I
## THE NATURE OF MODERN WORK

PART I

THE NATURE OF

MODERN WORK

"We find ourselves in an anxiety pandemic."

# 01 | Overwhelmed, Anxious, and Frustrated

In 2019, I was invited to speak at a conference of the top 200 bankers from a highly respected Swiss bank. It was their year-end celebration, where they showcase their performance and give awards to the best performers, and I was slated to go onstage right after that triumphant moment. As I walked into one of the most expensive hotels in Singapore, I could see that it must have been a good year. The place was decked out like a Chinese wedding, complete with fancy place settings and extravagant flower arrangements on large, round tables. Upbeat music was playing softly in the background. Everyone seemed to be in a good mood.

They wanted me to talk about how leaders could drive innovative business growth, and that is my area of expertise. So, in preparing my talk, I tried to put myself in their shoes.

Asia is home to many of the richest people in the world, and bankers manage that wealth. If I were one of them, I would probably have ten multi-billionaire clients, take home $3–4 million a year, and invest that money well. I would be in my mid-40s and have a family. I would be living comfortably in Singapore, one of the safest and most sophisticated cities in the world. In other words, I'd be sitting pretty—so why should I listen to some consultant who knows nothing about my business?

Good question. I could only come up with one plausible answer: if I showed a genuine interest in them as people, then maybe they would open their ears to me. So, I decided to start the session with a personal question—not my usual tactic, but it was worth a try. I figured that if I could get them to think about how blessed they are and how grateful they must be feeling, I could then turn their minds toward how they could help others.

So, when I got up to the podium, I asked, "In one word, how have you felt at work in the last 2 months?"

Everyone in the audience submitted their responses to the online survey tool, and we watched as the results popped up on the screen.

The top answer was… overwhelmed.

Number two… frustrated.

Number three… anxious.

Confused, I glanced through the rest of the results, searching for any indication of happiness or excitement. *Nothing.* I asked the audience if they were sure. Heads nodded around the room.

I was stunned. Scratch that—we were *all* stunned. Who had it better at work than the people in this room? They were high on the food chain, super successful, and well-rewarded for their efforts. And yet, even after their best year *ever*, they were not content. They were overwhelmed, frustrated, and anxious.

So, we started unpacking their answers. They told me they felt like everything was out of their control—the systems around them had them tied up in knots. They had lost all perspective on their lives. Despite how good their jobs looked on paper, their day-to-day experience was miserable.

This wasn't just a problem for these people as individuals—it was a problem for the company, too. It is not humanly possible to be overwhelmed and innovative at the same time; creativity and anxiety cannot coexist.

How could the company hope to grow, much less innovate, with its leaders and top performers constantly in this state?

And if these wealthy, senior people felt this way, what about the rest of the workforce?

## Stuck or Lost

Since then, I've had the same conversation with more than 3,000 leaders across various industries: oil and gas, consumer goods, hospitality, food, healthcare, government, and more. I asked them to describe, in one word, how they've felt at work in the last 2 months. Across the board, the answer is the same: *overwhelmed*, *frustrated*, and *anxious*.

Hearing their stories took me back to my early career, when I was an engineer fresh out of college, working on an engine factory floor. As a trainee, I stood at one machine, repeating the same three actions over and over in 35°C heat. At the end of each day, I went home and lay down, exhausted but blissful. My job was done. I had hit my targets for the day. From that moment until my next shift, there was absolutely nothing for me to do—zero baggage from work to home.

What most white-collar workers experience today is the *opposite* of that feeling. Every morning, you wake up weighed down by everything left unfinished and all the people who are depending on you. Your day is packed with work and meetings from sunup to sundown, yet you rarely see progress. There is no closure, no sense of 'done'. So many people are involved in every decision that even the simplest ideas take months to execute. Your efforts feel so dispersed that nothing seems to move the needle. It's like you're on a treadmill where someone is cranking up the speed and the slope at the same time... and at the end of each day, you have nothing to show for it but exhaustion.

There is no finish line. Your phone pings round the clock. And since COVID forced you to work from home, whatever boundaries you once had have been erased—no commute, no lunch break, not even a walk from your desk to the conference room. Is it any wonder that anxiety and depression have become the norm?

But you put up with it because you have a mortgage to pay, kids to put through college, and perhaps parents to take care of. You feel like it's too late to quit and pursue something more meaningful. Abandoning your current path would mean starting over from the bottom of the ladder with outdated skills—and you just can't afford to do that.

Or maybe you're at the start of your career, and the problem isn't that you have no choice—it's that you have too many. When my generation started working, we were assigned a manager who was expected to coach us and help us succeed. These days, young graduates do one project with one boss, and 2 months later, move on to something and someone else. There's no anchor, no constant, no one looking out for you. Meanwhile, you scroll through social media, seeing the interesting and glamorous things everyone else is doing. You wonder if you should go teach English in Cambodia, start your own business, or at least look for a better job.

It doesn't help that you're working remotely. You don't develop real relationships at work, so you feel invisible, which makes it much harder to sell yourself in the marketplace of skills. You never truly feel like you're part of the company, so it's easy to leave, and you end up jumping from one job to another. It's like swimming in open water—no lanes, no landmarks, no idea which way to go.

A huge portion of the white-collar workforce feels exactly what I've described above. Whether you're just starting your career and feeling lost or years into it and feeling stuck, the result is the same: you're overwhelmed, frustrated, and anxious. It's keeping you from doing your best work, and frankly, it's ruining your life.

## A Different Pandemic

We are in an anxiety pandemic.

I'm not the first person to point this problem out. In 2023, a study found that 68 percent of managers reported experiencing burnout—up from 43 percent the previous year (The Economist, 2023). That's an increase of more than 50 percent. What's going on here?

If you've been in the workforce for more than a decade, you probably know the answer in your gut: the nature of work has changed. The world is moving faster than it used to. Everything is more complex. The level of uncertainty is higher. We'll dig into this more in the next chapter, but for now, it's enough to say that the business environment has evolved, and the pressure has intensified.

So far, most organizations haven't figured out how to respond effectively. Those that have tried usually take one of two approaches.

The first approach is to treat burnout as a mental health issue and address it with benefits such as yoga classes, meditation spaces, and extra days off. Unfortunately, research shows that these solutions are largely ineffective, and it's easy to see why (Lowisz, 2023). We might try to disconnect from the chaos for a few minutes or days, but we never forget that it's waiting for us, piling up higher with every minute we're gone. In my case, even when I took time off for my mother's funeral, my mind kept straying to the emails I needed to send upon my return. No amount of mindfulness or rest can stop reality from crashing down the moment we get back to work.

The other approach is to solve burnout through organizational structure and management practices. I went down this path for several years. It started in 2017, when my firm had the opportunity to create a global center of excellence in partnership with the Singapore government. The focus of choice for this new center was "the future of work."

We wanted to figure out how organizations could keep up with the accelerating pace of change. Big companies struggled to adapt with wave after wave of new technology, rapidly evolving consumer preferences, and the constant threat of newer, more nimble competitors. So we explored strategies to help them make decisions and take action faster—for example, by reorganizing them into small teams. Our research focused on how leaders should plan and execute these major structural transformations to increase their organizations' agility.

At the SingularityU Thailand Summit in 2018, I gave a talk about this topic. Afterward, a journalist approached me. She said these ideas were well and good for corporate leaders and consultants, but what about individual employees? How can the average person function better in this new world of work?

I didn't have an answer for her. For all my fretting over how companies and governments would navigate the future, I hadn't thought about the individual at all. A few months later, at that private banker conference, it became clear that this was a major oversight. The future of work was already happening, and it was a major threat to the well-being of employees, and therefore, to the success of their companies. Most employees had no real control over organizational structure or management practices. If they had to rely on those solutions to liberate themselves from being overwhelmed, frustrated, and anxious, they would be waiting a long time.

## Human Agency

I wanted to discover if there are any individuals in the workforce who are consistently burnout resistant, and ask them – *what makes you different?*

To answer this question, I looked at the outliers—the people who were *not* burning out despite working under the same chaotic conditions as everyone else. There always seemed to be a few in every organization.

While others were **struggling**, these outliers seemed to be **thriving**.

How did they do it? What made them capable of handling the complexity, pace, pressure, and mess without breaking a sweat?

Well, I found it. Consistently. Every single time.

The answer, is, in one word, **agency**: our internal sense of power and control over our lives at work.

People with high agency feel like masters of their world. They have a strong sense of purpose and ownership over their work, so they get real joy and fulfillment from doing it. They're able to roll with the punches, focus on what matters, and marshal resources to get things done.

> High-agency individuals are self-motivated, self-directed, and, perhaps, most importantly, self-correcting.

On the flip side, people with low agency feel like victims, with no power or choice over anything at work. Everything is happening *to* them, and they're just trying their best to keep up. Each hiccup or change in the winds is another weight on their back, and they feel helpless to stop it.

I found unexpected theoretical basis of this idea in the world of psychology. When cognitive behavioral therapists talk about anxiety—which, as we've seen, is a major component of this burnout epidemic—they often refer to the "anxiety equation", a concept well known among cognitive behavioral therapy (CBT) practitioners (Tsatiris, 2022).

The simplest form of the equation is this:

$$Anxiety = \frac{Perceived\ Danger}{Perceived\ Ability\ to\ Cope}$$

In the context of modern work, what's the danger being perceived all around the world across all industries? *Uncertainty*. And what skill set gives people the ability to cope with uncertainty? *Agency*. In other words…

$$Anxiety = \frac{Uncertainty}{Agency}$$

Finally, it became clear why the organizational solutions consultants like me had been advising were not working. Building better support systems, creating safe spaces at work, providing career guidance, and making company structures more flexible and efficient—all these efforts focused on the *numerator* of that equation. The goal was to reduce uncertainty.

These efforts are well-intentioned and may benefit employees, but they won't stop the tides of change. The major drivers of rising uncertainty around the globe—technology, politics, economics, and social dynamics—aren't going away anytime soon. There are multiple major armed conflicts in the world right now; the market volatility index is at an all-time high, and with the unfolding move to AI at work, someone as prescient as Bill Gates has warned that within the next decade, advances in artificial intelligence will **render humans unnecessary** "for most things" in the world.

This combination of technological, social, political, and economic volatility is unprecedented in our lifetime, and no organizational effort can fully counter these forces.

In short, trying to reduce uncertainty is a fool's errand.

The cycles of change and disruption today are measured in weeks and months, not years and decades, ensuring a constant sense of anxiety in every boardroom in every sector.

Given this sustained high uncertainty in the environment around us, the only lever left to pull, in order to maintain our balance and find new pathways to progress, is our own human agency.

... the only lever left to pull is human agency.

You might think that agency is a function of your job title, your boss, or your organization's policies. It's not. Time and again, I've seen high-agency people working side by side with low-agency people under the exact same circumstances. I've met low-agency executives and high-agency interns. Agency is both a mindset and a skill, and you can develop it no matter where you work, who you work for, or what your job is.

That's what this book will teach you, with ten simple rules—rules designed to empower, not constrain you.

## Three forms of agency

These rules are grouped into three categories. The three categories of agency are personal, social and growth.

Think about personal agency as the exact opposite of victimhood— a constant feeling that the steering wheel at work is in your hands at all times. Your goals, aspirations, short-term focus, definition of success ... all these owned and managed by you, aligned with the expectations of the enterprise, of course, but always belonging to you.

Social agency is best defined as a contrast. Collaborating with people who are similar to you and think in the same way is easy. Social agency is the confidence and skill to collaborate with a wide range of humans who are different from you, to the extent that probably, *you don't get them* and *they don't get you.*

The third category is growth agency. Most individuals consider career growth as a vertical move in the same area of specialization— a promotion to become a more senior practitioner or a leader of other practitioners. High growth agency involves defining learning and growth horizontally, not vertically—finding the confidence to step out of your comfort zone of expertise, and expanding the radius of your know-how to adjacent domains.

The first four (Part II of this book) focus on your **personal agency**, or your individual sense of control over your daily work life. The next three rules (Part III) address your **social agency**, or your ability to make the most of your relationships with other people at work. The final three rules (Part IV) focus on **growth agency**, or your power to drive your own growth at work. While these rules are designed for individuals, in Part V, we'll explore how leaders can use them to cultivate a high-agency organization.

When you cultivate these three skills—personal agency, social agency, and growth agency—everything will change. You won't feel stuck anymore. You won't feel lost. You won't feel like you're hanging on by your fingernails.

You will rediscover what it means to thrive work.

## Breaking the Thin String

The common thread tying these rules together is that *you* have to be in charge of *you*. There will always be issues with your work environment and the people in it, but 90 percent of the power you need, you can take on your own. Your overwhelm may seem to come from what's around you, but the cure will come from within you. That's why I designed these rules to apply to any job level and require no organizational change or permission from your boss.

> Your overwhelm may seem to come
> from what's around you, but the
> cure will come from within you.

Still, you're probably thinking this won't work in your situation. It could work for some people, but not at your company, not with your boss, and not in your job.

That's usually the first thing I hear when I introduce these ideas. However, my research shows little correlation between the agency people feel and their environment. At the same company, on the same team, there can be people who feel powerless and people who thrive.

This reminds me of the way they tame wild elephants in Thailand. When an elephant is first captured, it is restrained with thick ropes to prevent it from breaking free. But as the elephant learns that its efforts are futile, the captors gradually replace the thick ropes with smaller ones—until, eventually, the huge animal is held by nothing more than a thin string. By then, it does not even try to escape anymore.

You may think you have a thick rope around your leg, but it's probably just a string. Maybe I'm wrong—but all I ask is you give agency a chance. Try these rules and see what happens. You might be surprised to discover that you're capable of far more than you expected.

> You may think you have a thick rope around
> your leg, but it's probably just a string.

In fact, I bet you'll find that agency is like toothpaste: once it's out of the tube, you can't put it back in. In my experience, people who start on this journey just keeps growing. It's like replacing walls with windows or unlocking new levels in a video game—it's hard to regress.

This journey looks different for everyone. I've seen someone struggling to manage a $500,000 book of business multiply it fivefold in less than a year, without breaking a sweat. I've seen someone grow their side hustle until it earned twice as much as their full-time job. I've seen someone drive major policy changes in their company and get singled out as a high-potential future leader.

You don't have to aim for anything so dramatic. The goal isn't to become a superstar. It's to contribute more value at work in less time, with less stress, so you have the time and energy for whatever matters in your life.

## My Personal Journey with Agency

It wasn't until I began implementing these rules for myself and my team that I fully understood their power. It was the beginning of the COVID era, and I was deeply concerned about keeping the team together without face-to-face interaction. Consulting work is challenging; we deal with long hours, tight timelines, lots of pressure, and frequent changes in priorities. With the transition to remote work, I worried that engagement would nosedive and that people would leave. My team was young and inexperienced, so they didn't have deep ties to the firm yet, and their high level of talent meant there was no shortage of other job opportunities for them.

I couldn't have designed a more difficult test for these rules. Our face-to-face time dropped to zero just as our business was growing, so we had to change all our ways of working to meet the demand. Everyone was spending long days at home in front of their laptops—perhaps the least ideal scenario for making work a joyful experience. And yet, thanks to our commitment to cultivating agency, our core team stayed together throughout the COVID period. Even more surprisingly, our levels of engagement, motivation, and closeness actually went *up*.

I didn't have to search for evidence of this with a magnifying glass. It was apparent in how my team started taking initiative without waiting for my instructions or permission. They reached out to collaborate with peers proactively. They started interviewing candidates for new positions before I finalized the headcount. They helped clients solve problems before the clients even brought the issue up to me. I could go on and on about the ways they took ownership over the work.

This was when the word "agency" came to my mind. Before this, we had been a high-performing team in terms of talent, but there had been much more weight for me to pull as a leader. I used to spend a lot of time driving the agenda, getting people aligned, and keeping them motivated. Now, it was almost unnerving how little they seemed to need that from me.

At first, self-doubt crept in. I wondered if people were doing things on their own because they thought I would get in the way or disapprove. But I soon realized it had nothing to do with me. It was simply a natural outcome of higher intrinsic motivation from everyone on the team. They didn't need so much external direction from me anymore—they just needed my insight and resources. This stunned me. If someone had told me that, during COVID, I would need to be *less* intense and active as a leader, I would have thought they were crazy. But that's exactly what happened.

The benefits extended to the business side of things as well. Before COVID, our work was almost always delivered to clients through in-person workshops. Suddenly, that became impossible. It's easy to imagine that people in that situation might worry about the future of their jobs and the business. They might feel overwhelmed as they try to learn the new remote work tools while keeping up with client demands.

None of that happened. My team seemed to master new skills overnight and share them with each other organically. Within a couple of weeks, we had developed a program called *Virtual First* to train our own people and our clients on how to operate in a virtual environment. Instead of adopting a victim mentality, my team saw this moment as a huge opportunity. They took the biggest possible shock to our business and transformed it into an offering that led to massive growth.

In the end, the greatest benefit wasn't for the business or for me as the team leader—it was for all of us as human beings. Near the height of the lockdowns, one team member suggested holding a team reflection session to check in on how everyone was coping. I had planned to lead it, but another team member volunteered to take over so I could just participate. It turned out to be one of the most caring, human, and mindful hours we had ever spent as a team—and I didn't even come up with the idea or led it. It was such a novelty for me to sit back and watch my team work together and uplift each other. In that moment, it became clear that work was not a drain for us; it was a source of strength, fulfillment, and **joy**.

None of this would have happened if we hadn't become a high-agency team. When the COVID lockdowns began, I fully expected to spend the next few months struggling to hold onto an increasingly disengaged team. Instead, my team brought their A-game. Their energy, creativity, and commitment were higher than ever. It all came from them, without me even asking.

That's what agency does. It charges your batteries. It lights you up. It transforms your entire approach to work, and therefore, your experience of work. And that's the real point—not just that you give your best effort at work, but that you *want* to give your best effort because you *love* your work.

So, if you're ready to turn your overwhelm, frustration, and anxiety into *joy*, turn the page.

"In modern work the straight path is no longer the path to success."

# 02 | What Is Modern Work?

I t was around 2015 that I felt the first hints of a sea change in the world of work. At the time, I was working for Korn Ferry, the world's largest executive search firm, so I had a pulse on the business leadership world. No one was talking about "the future of work" yet, but they were talking a lot about change, adaptability, and agility. We had finally gotten past the global financial crisis, and Silicon Valley, in particular, was thriving.

These young, fast-growing companies were leading the way in workplace innovation. Books like *Work Rules!* by Google's VP of People and Operations, Laszlo Bock, were making a huge splash. Laszlo said that everyone—not just company leaders—should think and act like founders, and everything else would follow from there. It was the first book I encountered that advocated an owner mindset for employees.

This new thinking was a major departure from the traditional management philosophies that had grown out of longstanding blue-chip companies like General Electric, Honeywell, and Johnson & Johnson. Their playbooks were geared toward the planned development of people and their careers, shaping them over time for roles that generated value. They focused on equitable performance management, training, and compensation, relying on managers to motivate and engage their employees.

This thesis of traditional work can be traced, in part, to the armed forces. Models used at West Point and other military academies were designed to deploy large groups of people and build loyalty to an organization (Cappelli and Tavis, 2016). By the mid-twentieth century, these models translated well to big corporations. Jack Welch, the renowned CEO of General Electric, built on those structures with management techniques designed to drive continuous improvement, such as performance-based compensation and the rank-and-yank system (i.e., regularly removing and replacing the lowest-performing employees).

This playbook worked pretty well for a long time, but we are now in a new era. With AI, possibilities that seemed unthinkable just 5 years ago are now a reality. Take Mistral, for example—a company that has developed a large language model capable of competing with ChatGPT. They achieved this in just 10 months with only 17 employees, and the company was valued at $6 *billion* when the product launched (Cordon, 2024). Sam Altman, CEO of OpenAI, believes it's only a matter of time before we see the first one-person, billion-dollar company (Confino, 2024).

What does this mean for employees? Massive fragmentation at work and the end of large, regimented organization with planned career paths and jobs for life—that was the context for the traditional management style, but in the new era of explosive startups and rapid change, that playbook is simply too rigid. The old ways of running a company—and the old paths to career success that went along with them—no longer work.

Some people look at this as the end of civilization. I take the opposite view: this shift has created powerful opportunities for anybody with the courage and motivation to seize them. To understand why this is true—and what to do about it—we first need to explore the four key shifts that make modern corporate work fundamentally different from what it was in the past.

## Shift #1: Hierarchy to Marketplace

In 2010, I met Bob Eichinger, creator of the world-renowned executive development program at Pepsi, over sushi in Minneapolis. He was one of the foremost thinkers on developing and managing human capital. After leaving Pepsi, he had started his own talent development consulting firm. By this time, he had retired and sold his firm to Korn Ferry, where I was then working. Everyone at Korn Ferry said I *had* to meet Bob—that we would really get along.

They were right. We spent more than 2 hours talking about the future of human capital. This was well before my focus shifted to the evolution of work, but he had already been thinking about it. In his view, moving forward, the world would be very different from the "factory" model of talent that had been prevalent for so long. Of all the things he said, what struck me most was his insistence that the corporate world wasn't learning enough from other fields of creativity and high performance, like sports and entertainment.

The factory model was all about titles and hierarchies. Your value in an organization was determined by your position in the pyramid and the number of people you managed. But you could be an extremely successful professional football player, actor, or artist without managing 15 other people. The difference was that, in those professions, value was tied to *skills*, not job roles. Bob predicted that to keep up with a rapidly changing world, corporations would have to adopt this model, and their hierarchies of authority would transform into networks of skills.

That's exactly what is happening. In a jobs-based organization, major changes in the business environment usually require a major restructuring. This involves hiring consultants, reassigning employees, retraining them, rebuilding operating teams, and losing some valuable employees. For a 20,000-person company, that might take 12—18 months and cost $5–10 million, not counting the disruption and opportunity cost, which could add up to $100 million or more. If major changes occur more than every 5 years, this process becomes cost-prohibitive.

That's when it makes sense to shift to a skills-based model, which is more flexible. Skills function like Lego blocks that can be rearranged more easily, allowing the company to adapt to change faster and with less disruption. Few companies have fully transitioned, but many are still trying to move in this direction, especially in fast-paced industries like technology.

The marketplace of skills is so beneficial for these organizations because the half-life of technical skills has fallen dramatically. And by half-life, I mean the number of years a particular skill remains relevant in the market. When I went to college in the early 90s, the half-life of skills was about 25 years. Today, it's down to 4 years—and still falling. With generative AI, it's not even 1 year. As the CEO of a top tech company put it, even their most experienced data scientists are having to unlearn everything they know and acquire a whole new set of data skills (which is even harder than learning from scratch).

In a hierarchical organization, you're told and taught what to do, and as you progress, you teach those same things to younger people. But when the half-life of skills is this short, that's organizational suicide.

More experienced employees won't necessarily be more knowledgeable or more valuable than new ones. I recently saw a demo on generative AI by a fresh college graduate that was better than what my company's senior data scientists could do. A marketplace of skills would better utilize that kid's abilities—and compensate him more fairly—than a hierarchical organization would.

In this new type of organization, careers start to resemble those of a Hollywood actor rather than climbing a corporate ladder. For the time it takes to make a movie (let's say 2 years), thousands of people bring together diverse skills: creative, technical, logistical, financial, and more. Many are working with each other for the first time. They collaborate for a finite period to produce perhaps a 2-hour film, and then they disband, each moving on to a new project with different people.

In this industry, the typical path is not linear. The most successful individuals find highly creative ways to expand and monetize their skills. Many actors branch out into modeling, directing, or producing. Some become venture capitalists or create powerful brands, like Gwyneth Paltrow's *Goop*. Reese Witherspoon is a particularly interesting case; she started a wildly successful (and lucrative) book club that promotes promising books in exchange for movie rights options.

The corporate workplace is inexorably moving in this direction. Is that good or bad? Probably a bit of both. In a marketplace of skills, you can rise faster than in a hierarchy—if you prove your value. There's also much more freedom to find a truly satisfying career path. However, no one will lay that path out for you. You'll have to seek out opportunities and "sell" your skills to those who need them. Hollywood actors have agents to help them—you don't. That's precisely why it's important to develop your own sense of agency.

## Shift #2: Physical and Time Boundaries

The dissolution of boundaries around work has been brewing since the early days of the Internet. Every technological leap made it easier to separate work from the physical office—home computers, laptops, PDAs, smartphones. By 2019, many knowledge workers routinely extended their workdays beyond office hours, taking work home and responding to communications at any time and from anywhere.

Then COVID hit, and remote work became the norm rather than the exception. In some ways, this was a good thing. In big cities with horrible traffic, not having to commute can save up to 4 hours a day, which is life-changing. For some, remote work also provides a flexible schedule that better fits their lifestyle. For the most part, we didn't see the major drop in productivity that some had expected with working from home.

But as we adjusted to the "new normal," it became clear that remote work had its drawbacks as well. One of these is the lack of psychological space between work and personal life. When your work is never really done (as is common in most white-collar jobs) and you never really leave the office, it's easy for the demands and stress of your job to linger over your head 24/7. You *could* be working at any time, so you feel like you *should* be working all the time. Meanwhile, when you're actually supposed to be working, it's easier than ever to get distracted by pets, kids, partners, roommates, errands, snacks—not to mention temptations like naptime and Netflix.

Plus, employers have found that remote work can undermine culture in subtle ways. Digital communication simply isn't the same as face-to-face interaction. No matter how much time you spend on Teams and Zoom, relationships tend to become more transactional, weakening teamwork, collaboration, and creativity. New employees struggle to build connections with others at the company, making it hard for them to develop a sense of belonging or loyalty. All these have a real impact on both employee satisfaction and business outcomes.

According to a Deloitte white paper (Roy et al., 2020), about 45 percent of work activities can be permanently done remotely with little downside. For any given person in an organization, this probably includes some portion of their work but not all. Now that it's safe to return to the office, a hybrid work situation has emerged, with many people splitting their time between remote and in-person work.

While this may seem like the best scenario for everyone, in practice, it often turns out to be the worst. The reason comes down to attention. When everyone on a team is remote, each person can set up a work environment and communication routine that allows them to focus. The same is true when everyone is in the office. But when some are remote and others are in person, things get messy. Imagine a meeting where three people are in the office, one is at home, one is at an airport, and one is at a Starbucks with a weak connection… It's easy to see how attention can become fragmented. In my experience, I've found this so unproductive that in any meeting where some are face-to-face and others are online, we all just switch to online. Everyone has to be in the same medium for communication to be effective.

There's no simple solution to this. Many CEOs would prefer to have everyone in the office, while many employees would prefer to work entirely remotely. This tension means that hybrid work is likely here to stay, and modern knowledge workers will need to find ways to navigate its challenges.

## Shift #3: Lifespan of a Job

According to LinkedIn, Generation X spends 4 to 4.5 years in each job role. For Millennials, this drops to about 2 years, and for Gen Z, it's just 7 months. People entering the workforce today can expect to experience at least six or seven career shifts of varying magnitudes throughout their working lives.

In some parts of the economy, like tech startups, this has been the norm for some time. But for most white-collar workers today, it's a new reality. Back in my day, it was considered crazy for someone to have even *one* major career turn. A friend of mine took early retirement from a successful banking career, got a master's degree in data science, and started his own company focused on financial trading algorithms. To my generation, he's a pioneer making bold moves and taking big risks… but in the new paradigm of modern work, career changes like his are becoming the rule rather than the exception.

Many people—especially those of us over 40—are not ready for this amount of change. Even if you want to stay on your career path, the environment around you will keep changing. If you don't proactively evolve with it, you'll be left behind, no matter how successful you've been in the past.

Take the case of a major electronics retailer I worked with recently. Most of their top executives have spent their whole careers at the company, usually having worked their way up through a single division. Now, the company is struggling to keep up with more innovative competitors, and the CEO is starting to realize that the C-suite's lack of diverse experience is part of the problem. If the company wants to survive, some of those loyal executives will have to go.

That's an extremely hard pill to swallow. Imagine being taught that the formula for career success was to work hard, perform well, and commit to becoming the very best in one area at one company. You've lived by this mantra for over 30 years, and it has worked so far. You've reached the top of the ladder, believing the final decade of your career— your peak achievement and your legacy—is secure… only to find out that actually, you're *not* valued, you're *not* safe, and you don't fit anywhere anymore.

In modern work, the straight path is no longer the path to success— it's not even an option anymore. The world around us is changing quickly, and if you don't adapt by choice, you'll be forced to change, which is terribly unpleasant. This happened to factory workers when robotics and automation entered the picture. It happened to journalists when the transition from print to digital disrupted the business models of newspapers and magazines. It's happening to Hollywood writers as the industry grapples with the rise of streaming platforms (hence the 2023 strike). And it's happening to programmers, designers, writers, lawyers, and countless others as the capabilities of artificial intelligence skyrocket. In all these cases, those who fail to evolve are the ones who end up out of a job and out of options.

This change is happening so fast that none of our career guidance or training is geared for it. There's been plenty of conversation about upskilling and reskilling the existing workforce in *reaction* to these changes, but not much focus on *preparing* people to expect and navigate a career full of twists and turns. It's unlikely that your university or company will teach you the importance of proactively adapting to change—which is one of the reasons I felt compelled to write this book.

> There's been plenty of conversation about upskilling and reskilling the existing workforce in *reaction* to these changes, but not much focus on *preparing* people to expect and navigate a career full of twists and turns.

## Shift #4: Teaming

As a consultant, I've spent many years guiding large companies through major transformations. Looking back at the projects I worked on 6 or 7 years ago, CEOs typically worked with no more than three vendors on an effort like that: strategy, technology, and personnel management. Today, if the business is even slightly complex—for example, insurance—those vendors have multiplied. At one company I'm working with, it's *eighteen*. There are multiple strategy partners, tech partners, specialists in niche areas like procurement, and more—many of whom are competitors within their own industries.

In situations like this, old-fashioned teamwork isn't enough. That's where a relatively small, stable group of people collaborate closely by spending a lot of time together and getting to know each other well—like a sports team. However, when the "team" consists of 18 vendors, each with multiple people working on the project whose identities and roles may change over time, that simple model no longer fits.

What's really happening there is "teaming"—a concept popularized in the book, *Teaming: How Organizations Learn, Innovate, and Compete in the Knowledge Economy*, by Edmondson (2012). Teaming is the ability of a fluid group of people to align around a common purpose and collaborate to achieve a goal. It's about working together even when you don't know each other well and the team is constantly changing. In short, it's teamwork on the fly, and it doesn't happen naturally or effortlessly. Without the right systems, skills, and mindset for teaming, these complex projects can go quite poorly indeed.

It's not just that teams are getting more complex; the rise of work methods like Agile has also dramatically increased the proportion of total work done by teams rather than individuals. A typical Agile team includes at least five functions: business/product, customer experience, solution design, development, and testing. In a pre-Agile world, these people worked separately within their own functions and handed the project off to each other in a fairly linear way. The business person would decide what features were needed, then pass that list to the customer experience person, who would test it with customer focus groups. Once the list was refined and approved, it would be handed off to the solution designer, who would determine the data algorithms, buttons, and other components needed to create the features. From there, the developer would create the solution, and then pass it to the tester.

The Agile revolution showed that if you bring these five people together and give them end-to-end responsibility for the product, you get better communication, faster feedback loops, and greater creativity. This results in a much better product in significantly less time. Shifting the work from the individual to the team also benefits management, as the teams are responsible for coordinating and managing themselves. They're essentially self-correcting.

One of my banking clients fully embraced this approach. Their mantra is: "You build it, you maintain it; it breaks, you fix it." Before this shift, most employees experienced a mix of working alone and collaborating with others throughout the day. Now, for most employees, almost their entire day is spent working with others. Things get especially hectic when multiple teams need to coordinate, which leads to a surge in the amount of communication required to get things done. None of this means their individual work has disappeared—it just means they end up doing it at 8:00 or 9:00 PM, after the incessant flow of communication has calmed down—and their mental batteries are drained.

This dramatic change in the quantity and complexity of team-based work has happened so fast that most organizations haven't yet adapted. According to research by Microsoft (2023), on average, more than half the workday is consumed by communication, leaving 68 percent of people feeling like they don't have enough uninterrupted focus time for productive work. Survey respondents identified inefficient meetings as the number one obstacle to productivity, with "too many meetings" ranking third.

What's clear is that the need for greater communication isn't going away. It's driven by fundamental changes in the business environment and the world at large, and we'll all have to find ways to adapt.

## Agency Won't Happen By Accident

The fact that these four shifts were happening became clear to me around 2017, but the 3 years of COVID were the straw that broke the camel's back. These trends accelerated massively, and changes that were once visible primarily in Silicon Valley and the management consulting world are now appearing in every industry. In many ways, what I learned in business school—focus on one job at a time, keep the boss happy, put your head down and grind to make senior partner, then hang on for dear life and retire at 55—is now the opposite of what we all need to practice at work.

Unfortunately, what I was taught 20 years ago is still being taught today. Those ideas aren't just outdated—they're dangerous. Following that advice is a surefire way to get blindsided by change, and it certainly won't help you manage the overwhelm, frustration, and anxiety that have become the norm in white-collar work worldwide. As I've learned over the last 4 years, only agency can help you navigate this.

What especially concerns me is that when I interviewed people with high agency, I noticed a pattern in their personal histories that mirrored my experience. After finishing my MBA, I decided to go into consulting. On my very first project, the project manager, director, and senior consultant all left suddenly, and I ended up running the project myself. This allowed me to build a great relationship with the partner, who later recommended me for my next project. That project had me advising the owner of Wipro, one of the richest people in India—just 6 months out of grad school. After that, I was assigned to help create a 30-year vision for *India Today*, the most influential periodical in the country at the time.

At the end of that wild first year, I happened to bum a cigarette off the Managing Director of the Asia Pacific region at my firm, who was visiting India. As we chatted over a casual smoke, he found out I was an engineer and told me the firm was planning to start a practice building online HR portals for clients—did I know how to do that? I sure did. So, he brought me to Singapore to set up that practice. Two years later, they asked me to run the whole practice across Southeast Asia. That experience perfectly laid the foundation for my later work—building leadership centers and creating leadership consulting practices.

There's a pattern here: early in my career, I got lucky and made the right connections with the right people at the right time. I was fortunate to be hand-picked by leaders and given the opportunity to take on something huge and watch it succeed. I learned that I was capable of handling big responsibilities, big challenges, and big risks. There were plenty of scary bumps along the road, but in those early years, I proved to myself that I could recover from setbacks and come out stronger. I built a high sense of agency entirely by accident.

That's the same kind of story I have heard from many other high-agency people I interviewed over the last few years. However, that story is far less likely to unfold today. In a marketplace of skills, there's much more transparency, which leads to increased competition. Instead of using their intuitive judgment to pick someone out of the crowd, leaders are more likely to rely on data.

Perhaps that's a good thing (it's certainly more meritocratic). However, it does mean that high agency is unlikely to develop by accident. You'll need to be intentional about cultivating it for yourself—and that's exactly what we're about to do.

# 03 | Measuring Agency: The Thrive Index

Before you dive into developing your agency, there's one more question to answer: where are you starting from?

If we don't establish a good baseline, it's impossible to know for sure whether you're making progress, if you're backsliding, or if you need extra focus and support in certain areas. This is even more important for people in leadership roles, who are responsible for helping others increase their agency. How will you know if what you're doing is really working?

By measuring it, of course.

I know employee satisfaction surveys are nothing new. But the vast majority are focused on validating the organization's policies, processes, and programs—in other words, asking whether you (the employee) like me (the organization). They ask whether you like the cafeteria, the bonus program, your boss, your coworkers, the company's strategy… but they never really ask how *you* are doing. One particularly memorable engagement survey I found focused on measuring three key outcomes: whether employees speak positively about the company, whether they plan to stay at the company, and whether they strive to contribute to the company. It's supposedly a survey about employees, but the questions all revolve around the company.

I spent three decades in the corporate world without ever noticing how weird this was. It wasn't until I began this research on agency that I realized I had never seen a survey that simply asked employees how they were doing—and why. Are you thriving? Nobody knows.

When I started asking that question, most of the time the answer was NO. The reasons were rarely related to the organization's policies or programs. Instead, they were things like: *there's no meaning in my life; I'm bored; there's no one around that I enjoy working with;* or *I have no control over my work.* Among those who *were* thriving, their reasons boiled down to a few different things: freedom and independence; meaning and impact; and learning and growth.

Those concepts are a galaxy away from what's typically found in employee surveys. So, to measure agency, my team and I had to create a strikingly different kind of survey. We call it the *Thrive Index.* Take it now to get a baseline measure of your sense of agency—and your ability to thrive—at work.

## Measure Your Baseline

The Thrive Index has only seven questions. For each one, you choose a number from 0 to 10 that best reflects how you currently feel at work. At the end, you'll add up your score and see what it tells you.

### Control

*0: I feel overwhelmed, with little to no control over my choices and actions.*

*10: I feel focused, with full control and ownership over my choices and actions.*

This may seem closely tied to your level of seniority within your organization. However, I've known many senior executives who would score below a 5 on this because of the exploding number of stakeholders involved in every decision. At the same time, I try to ensure that even the entry-level analysts on my team score at least a 7 on this (and every) question. Of course, junior employees will always need to escalate some matters, but there's a lot they can do without asking for permission, given the opportunity.

## Meaning

*0: My work feels disconnected from what I find purposeful and meaningful.*
*10: My work is tightly linked with my purpose and deeply meaningful to me.*

This is perhaps the most important question in the survey, as you'll see in the next chapter. Getting meaning from your work *every day* is a high bar, and it's rare to find someone who scores a solid 10 here, but that's the ultimate goal. What's interesting, though, is that traditional employee engagement surveys *do* usually have a question about purpose. The difference is that it's not about *your* purpose—it's about whether you like the company's purpose. That's not the same thing, and even when employees agree with or like the company's purpose, their daily work may feel so disconnected from it that it has no bearing on their personal sense of purpose.

## Efficacy

*0: I put in a lot of effort at work, yet it does not reflect in my achievements.*
*10: I feel a strong connection between my efforts and my achievements at work.*

This is huge, and employee satisfaction surveys never address it. When you talk to people with "boring" jobs—laying bricks, for example—what really drives them is momentum. The work might be strenuous, repetitive, and dull, but they can *see* their progress in real-time. At the end of the day, they can stand back and be satisfied knowing they built something. On the other hand, many knowledge workers do very "interesting" work, but at the end of the day, they have no idea if they've laid another layer of bricks or just run in circles on a hamster wheel. They wonder what the point is of all this intellectual and creative effort if nothing comes of it. That's why momentum is an essential component of thriving at work.

## Energy

*0: I find my interactions at work to be a drain on my energy and enthusiasm.*
*10: I gain positive energy and enthusiasm from my interactions at work.*

The importance of this question is clear: if you're chronically exhausted, you're not thriving. For most people I talk to, work is a drain on their energy, not a source of it.

> . . . if you're chronically
> exhausted, you're not thriving.

They look outside of work for people and activities that help them recharge. But when you spend half of your waking hours each week at work, and additional time on other energy-draining activities like commuting, errands, and chores, there's little time left to recharge. The best way to solve this problem is to turn work into something that generates energy for you instead of only spending it.

## Belonging

*0: I find myself somewhat isolated and detached from others at work.*

*10: I feel a deep sense of attachment and belonging to people at work.*

In large organizations, real impact rarely comes from one person alone. It takes collaboration, usually across multiple functions, to do anything that makes a significant difference. So, when you feel disconnected from the rest of the organization, you also feel disconnected from that impact. You might excel in your particular area, but if you can't see how your work fits into the bigger picture, it will likely feel somewhat pointless. To thrive at work, it's crucial to feel a sense of belonging to the organization as a whole and to know that you have a purpose within it.

To thrive at work, it's crucial to feel a sense of belonging to the organization as a whole and to know that you have a purpose within it.

## Learning

*0: My work is repetitive with little opportunity to learn new skills and perspectives.*

*10: I am learning new skills and gaining new perspectives almost every day at work.*

This question is not about how much time you spend in training, workshops, or other formal learning situations. It's about whether you are learning through the course of your work—mastering the tools you use, becoming more knowledgeable in your field of expertise, gaining a deeper understanding of your users, etc. As I explain later in this book, continuous learning is essential for thriving, and there are much better ways to do it than by listening to a lecture.

## Growth

*0: I feel stuck—my professional confidence, influence and standing is not growing fast.*

*10: I am experiencing fast growth in my confidence, influence and professional standing.*

It's human nature to crave progress—especially when the possibilities for bigger and better things are all around us. Even for those who are perfectly content with their current work situation, it has become difficult to sit happily still when the world around them is rapidly changing. If they don't keep moving forward, they risk being left behind. This can be a major source of anxiety, which is why steady professional growth has become a prerequisite for thriving at work.

## Get Your Score

Add up the numbers you chose for each of the seven questions. Your total will fall somewhere between 0 and 70. Here's what that number tells you.

### 0-20: Struggling

If you're in this category, it is time to change. Reflect, understand, and create a shift in yourself and/or your environment. The level of stress you're experiencing could take a serious toll on your health. It's long overdue to do something different or find a new situation—anything to preserve your sanity and well-being.

### 21-40: Coping

You're not on the brink, but your situation is not sustainable in the long run. The negativity you're experiencing at work is likely already affecting your physical and mental health and spilling over into your personal life. Something needs to improve within the next –6 to 12 months, or you risk burning out.

### 41-60: Striving

For the most part, you're feeling good at work. Congratulations! That's something to celebrate. The next step for you is to think about elevating the areas that are a little low for you. You're also in an excellent position to help others learn how to thrive by developing their sense of agency.

### 61–70: Thriving

Scores this high are extremely rare. You're most likely the founder of your own company, where your work, passion, and life have merged into one. You probably don't need this book for yourself—just keep doing what you're doing. However, if you are in a leadership position, keep reading to learn how you can help others thrive in your organization.

## Our Results So Far

We've tested this with around 1,000 people at this stage, including partners I worked with at my firm. In each case, the average score ranged from 20 to 30, with around 20 percent struggling and less than 5 percent thriving.

The reaction is often some level of shock. There's usually a lot of nervous laughter—as in, *wow, I need to do something about this.* Most people are surprised they've never asked themselves these questions, and neither has their organization. They're startled by how bad their relationship with work really is.

There's a growing consciousness among business leaders that this is a serious problem. A Gallup study from 2020 found that employees who aren't thriving in their lives—even if they're "engaged" at work—pose a risk to the organization. They report significantly higher levels of stress, worry, anger, sadness, and burnout, and are much more likely to miss work for health reasons. Unsurprisingly, this significantly undermines their productivity (Harter, 2020).

That's why the executives I work with are so interested in the Thrive Index.

As companies restructure and downsize, their leaders are beginning to recognize the importance of caring for the employees who stay— especially when those people have to take on a bigger workload. There's a growing consciousness that we're entering a different era of work, one that requires companies to support their workforce in a different and better way.

> There's a growing consciousness that we're entering a different era of work, one that requires companies to support their workforce in a different and better way.

# PART II
# PERSONAL AGENCY

# PART II

## PERSONAL AGENCY

"Personal Agency is the opposite of victimhood."

Before we dive into the three rules around personal agency, we must first establish exactly what we're talking about here. What *is* personal agency?

Among the many knowledge workers I've known over the years, there are some who manage to create enormous impact with minimal stress. In that group, I can't think of anyone who felt like they were trying to achieve something for someone else. They all felt like they were working for themselves, despite the fact that only a handful of them were actually founders or leaders of their own companies.

Regardless of their position on the corporate ladder, they talked about their work as a personal mission, not something they did for the sake of their boss or the shareholders. Their aspirations were personal, and they took pride in their achievements. They see their work not as just doing a job, but as building a "franchise"—not a literal franchise, but something like a product, program, team, client base, or initiative. That word captures the high degree of ownership these people felt over their work *and* the awareness that it was part of a larger platform.

For example, one man I interviewed became the head of network at a telecoms company in South East Asia. Traditionally, the job is to keep the 4G/5G network running smoothly. It's all highly technical and maintenance-oriented, as you can probably imagine, even if you don't know anything about telecoms. However, this guy understood that the business customers were seeking more than just a reliable network. They wanted protection from hacking. They wanted to save money on cloud services by optimizing their data management. They wanted to grow their businesses through content.

A traditional head of network would have treated these issues as outside their scope. Instead, this executive chose to redefine his role by building a solution-oriented business that recognized the needs of his customers. So, as the infrastructure owner, he began partnering with other companies to solve these problems. Suddenly, his "franchise" was not just a cost center, as it had always been—it became a growth opportunity for the company.

Here's another example. A woman in real estate was given the responsibility to manage a sizable amount of land in Indonesia. The typical approach in that situation would be to develop it with the usual types of buildings—maybe shopping malls, offices, hotels, or residential condos. Nine out of ten people in her position would have followed that playbook. However, this woman wanted to use this opportunity to do something even more meaningful.

One of the biggest challenges in Indonesia is poor access to healthcare. People travel abroad even for minor checkups and procedures. There are also few medical schools, leading to shortages of doctors and nurses. So, she decided to build a biomedical hub on this land. No one told her to—the company would have been just as happy if she had built condos and a golf course. However, she took the initiative to envision a connected ecosystem where research, education, services, talent, and data all come together. She also initiated conversations with government agencies and international medical schools to make it possible.

This is what a high degree of personal agency looks like. These two individuals have taken quite ordinary jobs with clear playbooks and redefined them by incorporating the concept of building a franchise. They're not founders—they're working within a larger company. Still, they've claimed a high degree of ownership and control over their work.

It's worth noting that people with high personal agency often work even harder than their peers, yet they worry less, have higher motivation, and feel less pressured. That flies in the face of the idea that the key to avoiding burnout is setting boundaries on your job, making it smaller and less demanding. You don't need to do less. You just need to feel like what you do is *yours*—your own franchise, however big or small, within your organization. Whether you're an executive or an individual practitioner, the core idea is to take control of who you are and what you do.

That said, it's not about simply doing whatever you want. No matter where you are in the corporate hierarchy, you have expectations to meet and people to answer to. No one will just hand you the right to manage your own work life. If you want more trust and control, you must *earn* it by exceeding those expectations and demonstrating your ability to think expansively about the value you bring to the organization. The path won't necessarily be smooth or easy; the two people I mentioned earlier faced significant resistance from their superiors and colleagues. However, through persistence, they were able to redefine their roles that provided them with far more independence, meaning, and growth at work.

> If you want more trust and control, you must *earn* it by exceeding those expectations and demonstrating your ability to think expansively about the value you bring to the organization.

Ninety percent of the people I speak with have never thought about personal agency in their entire careers. If you woke them up in the middle of the night and asked what they were building at work, they wouldn't be able to answer. The vast majority of people see their goals as a set of external expectations they're just trying to meet. This is true for highly successful people, including some CEOs. Once you start looking at your work through that lens, you lose your internal compass and start to feel out of control and overwhelmed.

Nobody can fix that compass for you. The solution isn't in your external environment; it's an internal orientation. It comes down to the direction you choose to take, where you focus your attention, and the stories you tell yourself.

It's true that gaining personal agency can be easier in some environments than others. Your company, team, and role certainly make a difference. You may feel there are many roadblocks to developing your personal agency, and that may be true. Still, your internal orientation is always within your control. It's your choice. You may not be able to fully manifest it as you'd like—for example, that telecoms executive I mentioned wanted to make big investments in cybersecurity as a service to other telcos, but the board of directors wouldn't allow it. They perceived his idea as a threat to their competitive position. He accepted this limit, but continued developing other areas where the board had bought in. Even with limitations, you *can* still make progress.

Similarly, personal agency is more important in some environments than in others. In organizations that operate as a marketplace of skills, personal agency is a prerequisite. Take consulting for example. New consultants coming into my firm must find their own place in the organization, choose projects to work on, and figure out how to grow their impact and network. Without personal agency, they'll be lost. However, in a strong hierarchy of authority, like the military, personal agency is less crucial for thriving. Clear orders are given, and you're obliged to follow them. But even so, every soldier has an internal story about why they do what they do, and the greater their sense of a personal mission and pride, the easier it is to persevere through adversity.

When I explain personal agency to people, they say it makes sense, but they're not sure how to do it. *Indro, you don't understand. I have too many bosses and too many expectations, and I already feel overwhelmed and boxed in from all directions. How do I work toward taking control and telling myself a different story?*

A lot of this pushback comes down to learned helplessness. Remember the story I told earlier about the elephants tied up with a thin string? Many people who have tried to take initiative and faced barriers start telling themselves a story: *The company doesn't care about me. I don't matter to the organization. I'm working for a paycheck. My manager sets the mandate and boundaries, and that's it.*

Once that narrative is set, it won't change without some trigger or process. Some would say that the best way to take control of your work is to follow your passion and quit your job to start your own business. I don't subscribe to that view; most people I meet can't afford to take that risk. When you have mouths to feed and obligations to fulfill, you need a different playbook.

That's where the rules of personal agency come in. In my career, I was fortunate to have mentors who pushed me to think this way from day one. In modern work, you probably won't be so lucky. Everyone is busy and overwhelmed. If your manager or mentor is in a chronic state of near-burnout, they won't be able to guide you this way. The skills to maximize your personal agency must come from within you—and that journey starts now. Let me get you started.

"High personal agency feels like having your hands on the steering wheel at all times."

# 04 | Rule #1: Bring Your Own Motivation

M ost organizations I work with suffer from the flawed hypothesis that employees are motivated primarily by external factors. They believe that with the right combination of targets, rewards, and punishments, they can drive people to do their best work. This mindset aligned perfectly with the theories of human behavior that were proposed and popularized in the early twentieth century.

Today, we know those theories are, at best, incomplete and, at worst, wildly inaccurate. As Daniel Pink explains in his book, *Drive*, external motivation is only one half of the equation—in most cases, the less important half (Pink, 2009). Internal motivation is often far more important and powerful, and it comes from a combination of three sources: autonomy, mastery, and purpose. Autonomy is your sense of independence and control over your choices. Mastery is the feeling that you're getting better and better at something every day. Purpose is the belief that what you're doing is meaningful and worthwhile.

These are the things that charge your mental and emotional batteries. Every day, you drain those batteries a little (or a lot), trying to solve problems, navigate conflicts, and meet other people's expectations. That's inevitable. And just like your phone, your brain has a finite amount of juice. You have to recharge it regularly for it to work properly. The question is: What replenishes your energy at work, where you spend most of your time each day?

I can promise that it's not some performance bonus or KPI goal. Carrots and sticks, no matter how finely tuned, won't change how you feel about your daily work experience. At best, they simply reward you for persevering through the stress and pressure; at worst, they add to it.

Internal motivators, on the other hand, *do* affect how you feel. They materially change your emotional state before, during, and after your working day. The same challenges may still exist—the intractable problems, clashes with coworkers, and infuriating strategic zig-zags won't magically disappear. However, strong internal motivation helps you bounce back from those things instead of being dragged down.

In short, you must bring your own motivation to work, because *nobody else will*. Despite their best efforts, your superiors *cannot* make you feel excited and energized about your work. That's entirely up to you.

---

In short, you must bring your own motivation
to work, because *nobody else will.*

---

This is the most important of all the rules because, without it, you won't have the energy or desire to tackle the rest of the playbook. However, most employees rarely think about where their motivation comes from or how to maximize it. Virtually no one—not even the most senior individuals—regularly asks themselves how to increase their autonomy, mastery, and purpose at work. Fortunately, there are three simple steps you can do to maximize your internal motivation.

## (1) Separate Your Identity from Your Job

How do you introduce yourself to new colleagues or clients?

If it's by your job title, that has to change. Your current job title doesn't even begin to capture your particular skill set or the value you bring to others in the context of your work. Your job is just the role you happen to be in at the moment, but *you* as a professional, are much more than that—you have your own personal history, interests, and goals for the future. Other people might have the same job title as you, but you bring something special to the table.

It's time to package all that into a unique narrative about who you are and what you're doing in the context of work. To be clear, this is *not* about your personal identity outside of work—your hobbies, family, pets, favorite foods, or anything else. It's about how you see yourself in the context of your career.

Articulating this is a powerful way to generate a sense of autonomy and purpose in your work life. When you start to consider your *whole* professional identity, it becomes clear that your current job is just one part of that identity. Your work can have meaning and purpose beyond the limits of your official job description. And when that job is just one piece of the puzzle rather than the whole, you're more likely to feel like you own that piece rather than it owning you.

That's why I insist that all my clients do this. Whatever you come up with doesn't have to sound glib or dramatic. It just needs to be unique, personal, and authentic. For example…

My job title is Lead Partner, but I like to say that I'm a career consultant, and my work lies at the intersection of technology and psychology.

The VP of Innovation at a major technology company says she brings data and creativity together to make social media less harmful.

An HR specialist at an insurance company says he's a people engineer—an engineer by background who brings engineering rigor and discipline into solving people's problems.

The CEO of a bank says he's an expert in listening to people with empathy and meeting them where they are.

You can see that all these examples are short and simple, yet they manage to convey much more about the person than their job title alone ever could. In more than one case, the descriptions they've chosen actually challenge the stereotypes associated with their job titles, which hints that there's more than meets the eye. If you were meeting these people for the first time and they introduced themselves this way, you might do a mental double take. You might look a little harder, listen a little closer, and be more interested in getting to know them.

But even more important is the impact these descriptions have on the people who created them. Instead of being defined by their job, they get to decide who they are as professionals and the unique value they bring to their current role and organization. In just a few minutes, and without changing anything about their work environment, they manage to materially increase their internal sense of control over their work life.

So, give this a try for yourself. How would you describe yourself as a professional *without* using your job title? Start by giving yourself at least 30 minutes to brainstorm and write freely, without editing. Ask yourself questions like:

- What are my areas of expertise or interest?
- What are my strengths as a professional?
- What makes me different from my colleagues?
- What do I care about achieving in my work?
- What is my approach or perspective?

Once you've written down your ideas on paper, you can choose the most important elements and craft a sentence or two that captures them concisely.

Then, *use* those words. Write them down and tape them to your desk. Read them every day. Put them in your work directory, LinkedIn profile, Slack account—anywhere you have a professional bio. And, of course, whenever you meet someone new in a work context, introduce yourself in this new way.

## (2) Move from KPIs to Aspirations

In most corporate environments, KPIs rule the day. You probably know exactly what you're expected to achieve at work, whether it's in terms of dollars in revenue, number of new customers, order fulfillment time, employee satisfaction rating, or some other metric. Those are goals, but they're not aspirations.

For example, my KPI in my job might be to build a XXX million USD business, but my *aspiration* is to bring agency to a billion people. These things are related but different. A KPI is a measurable goal that's tightly connected to the financial success of your organization, usually assigned to you by someone else. An aspiration, on the other hand, is a big-picture vision of the impact *you* want to make on the world through your work. The former is about hitting a target or checking a box; the latter is about striving for a purpose beyond yourself and your organization.

For example, I know a man on LinkedIn who grew up in Nepal with poorly educated parents. His aspiration is to build something that gives kids like him, in the most remote parts of the world, access to information about career options and opportunities. He manifests that by bringing LinkedIn to underprivileged communities. He has KPIs, too—things like the number of communities reached, the number of accounts created, and engagement on those accounts. His aspiration gives those numbers meaning. They're no longer just targets to hit; they're steps to take in service of his personal mission.

---

His aspiration gives those numbers meaning. They're no longer just targets to hit; they're steps to take in service of his personal mission.

---

That has a remarkably real impact on the energy he brings to work every day. I know that if I walked into any corporate office and asked people how they felt about their KPIs, the response would be a mix of shrugs, groans, and eye rolls. Nobody is fired up about their KPIs. The only way KPIs generate any response is through the promise of rewards for reaching them or punishments for failing to do so—classic extrinsic motivation.

Aspirations, on the other hand, generate *intrinsic* motivation. Your aspiration represents something you deeply care about, so you actually *want* to pursue it, not because someone told you to, but because it truly matters to you. Focusing on your aspirations recharges your batteries; it gives you the energy and desire to tackle the challenges of your work.

Everyone I've talked to who thrives at work has a clear aspiration. Here are a few more examples…

- A team leader in a food business aspires to minimize food waste.
- A project manager building schools in Southeast Asia aspires to give every child access to top-quality teachers.
- A cyber-security professional aspires to develop a new method to counter the threat of emerging cyber risks.
- A leader in a global career platform wants to help people in their late careers find their "third act"—a new phase that aligns with their passion.
- An HR professional in an oil and gas company aspires to put women in at least 30 percent of corporate board seats.
- A tech executive in a global company aspires to create a non-disruptive way for companies and employees to adopt AI.
- A leader at a bank in an emerging market wants to bring credit opportunities to people traditionally deemed not creditworthy.

What is your aspiration? In other words, what's the problem you want to solve? What's the difference you want to make?

In live workshops, I ask participants to think about that question in terms of four areas of their lives: health, wealth, work, and personal brand. The first three are fairly self-explanatory. I added the fourth because most people focus on their professional aspirations within the boundaries of their organization. Personal brand expands your thinking beyond that—to your identity and how you're perceived in the wider world.

Here is an example of what this might look like—it is based on a few different aspirations, curated to help you understand the frame.

| Health | Wealth |
|---|---|
| • Be able to run 10 km<br>• Normalize my blood pressure<br>• Lose 10 kg in body weight<br>• Improve mental well-being through reconnecting with the most important people in my life<br>• 2 years to get a clean bill of health (no medications) | • Double my sources of income<br>• Restructure my investments to generate an x% sustainable return<br>• Build a plan to be financially independent in 4 years<br>• Set up a contingency fund (rethink my insurance portfolio) |
| **Work** | **Personal Brand** |
| • Double the productivity of the team in 2 years<br>• Embed AI capacity and capability into product design to constantly move the needle on user experience<br>• Build an ecosystem of partners (startups) to create a capability community | • Feature in a Ted Talk<br>• Get my book published in 2 years<br>• Start a podcast with experts in my field<br>• 10X followers on social media platforms<br>• Teach a program at university |

If you start with health or wealth, you'll probably find it easier to get your mind in the frame of aspirations. These are two areas where people feel the desire for something more or better, but they don't have a concrete idea of what that looks like. Let's fix that right now. Remember, an aspiration is a big-picture vision that inspires and motivates you, not a New Year's resolution to go to the gym every day or save 10 percent of every paycheck.

So, what's your grand vision for your health? How do you want to feel physically and mentally? What do you want to be able to do? When you visualize yourself in great health, what do you see? Write it down.

The same goes for your wealth. How do you want to feel about your money? What do you want to be able to do with it? When you imagine yourself in your ideal financial state, what does that look like? Write it down.

Now that you're getting the hang of thinking in terms of aspirations, think about your professional life. What do you want to be able to do with your work? What impact do you want your career to make in the world? Write it down. Remember: think big, long-term, and inspirational. If what you're imagining is within easy reach, go *bigger*.

Finally, think about your life in the broadest sense: not just who you are at work but who you are *in the world*. That's your personal brand. What do you want to be known for? Who do you want to be to others? This might include creative pursuits, community involvement, philanthropy, adventures, hobbies… whatever is important to you.

To make sure you're on the right track as you define your aspirations, here are two questions to ask yourself.

## Will this aspiration bring me fulfillment even without external validation?

In other words, if no one else knew you had achieved your aspiration, would it still be rewarding and worthwhile to you? KPIs are the opposite of this; you only care about achieving them because if you do, you will be rewarded with a bonus, a promotion, or special recognition of some kind. Aspirations must be intrinsically rewarding—the fulfillment comes from within you, regardless of whether anyone else values your achievement.

*Do your aspirations align with each other and with your environment?* Aspirations work best when they're mutually reinforcing. For example, writing this book is part of my personal brand aspiration, and it aligns perfectly with my professional aspiration and my team's business goals. If I had wanted to write a cookbook instead, my book dreams would have been completely disconnected from my professional world. That's not wrong or bad, but it would make it much harder to support both aspirations, because the efforts that go toward one do nothing to advance—and might even undermine—the other.

Aspirations are meant to inspire, so keep them top of mind. Distill them down into clear, concise statements that you can put on your wall or keep in your wallet. Remind yourself each day that your efforts are aimed at something meaningful.

## (3) Focus on Your Superpower

If you watch someone swim 200 laps a day, it might seem incredibly boring from the outside. However, if you talk to that person, she'll say she's a competitive swimmer trying to beat her time, and it's the most motivating and rewarding thing she does every day. Yes, it's repetitive, but because she's laser-focused on honing every tiny detail—each stroke, each kick, each breath, each turn—it's anything but dull.

When I ask people what saps their motivation at work, they often complain about repetitive tasks. They hate to do the same tasks over and over again, whether it's crunching numbers, making sales calls, interviewing candidates, or updating project boards. The things they do most frequently are the ones they find most mind-numbing and energy-draining.

Those tasks may seem like a nuisance, but in fact, they're an opportunity for mastery. Anything you have to do repeatedly is something you can get a little better at every time—a little faster, a little more efficient, a little more perfect.

Athletes and artists know this all too well. Their ability to succeed depends on their willingness to do the same things repeatedly—imagine the basketball player doing countless free throws, the cellist playing endless scales. They never stop, not even when they've reached the top of their fields. They keep repeating these basic tasks with the utmost care and attention every single day, always seeking to execute them as flawlessly as possible. They're cultivating their superpowers.

What's your superpower? What are you trying to get better and better at every day? In the corporate world, nine out of ten people tell me they've never even thought about it. Either that, or they give me a long list of job tasks, none of which are particularly compelling. Almost no one is able to zero in on the one thing they're trying to master every day—the one thing that would set them apart from others.

My superpower is simplicity: taking complicated concepts and expressing them in simple, memorable, jargon-free narratives. My presentation slides have very few words, and sometimes, I spend a whole day making one slide. That's crazy in consulting—we give presentations all the time, and consultants often make 40 or 50 slides a day. They would call my way inefficient, but I believe in my way. I love the challenge of it, and my clients value it because they can understand more with less effort. I believe I can keep honing this skill for the rest of my life and never be "done."

A superpower isn't a traditional skill set like analysis or project management. It's something that sets you apart from your peers and that you can cultivate continuously through the daily activities of your work. It could be something like...

- Generating support and buy-in for ideas
- Solving any crisis with a cool head
- Getting more done with less
- Calming down teams in crisis and conflict
- Articulating the value of a business to investors
- Getting people with different perspectives to collaborate

These are just a few examples based on real people I know—the possibilities are endless.

The first two steps in this chapter focused on expanding your identity, but this step is a contraction. The goal is to identify the *one* skill you're dedicated to mastering every single day. This focus infuses everything you do with a new layer of purpose. Even the most mundane tasks become part of a continuous effort to become the best at something, motivating you to approach them with much more energy, intention, and passion. The bonus is that when you do this consistently for long enough, you actually *do* develop a superpower that makes you more valuable and competitive in your organization and field.

## Conclusion

As you can see, this chapter has not given you a long list of ways to charge up your motivation. There are just three simple steps: articulate your identity, define your aspiration, and focus on your superpower. Usually, it takes no more than a few hours to do these three steps, and that time investment can make a significant and lasting difference in how you feel about going to work every day.

The beauty of this is that anyone can do it, no matter what kind of work environment you're in or what constraints you face. However, few people ever do. We're not simply in the habit of taking the time to think about our work lives in such a structured way. It may even feel strange or uncomfortable, like working a muscle you've never exercised before. But if you take the time to do this simple process, you'll see how powerfully your own mind can shape your experience at work every day.

We asked all our principals at our firm to not only write these down, but create a short script and record their story on video. These short videos are now shared with everyone in the firm to understand the human being behind the title.

This is the first step to unlocking your personal agency. It's not a one-and-done process; your answers to the questions in this chapter will evolve over time, so you'll want to revisit them periodically. Allow yourself to grow and change direction when you need to. Just remember that you're the only one who can bring your motivation to work—no one else can do it for you.

# VISUAL SUMMARY : BRING YOUR OWN MOTIVATION

**Separate your identity from your job**

MY IDENTITY

▲
▲

MY JOB ROLE

**Move from KPIs to aspirations**

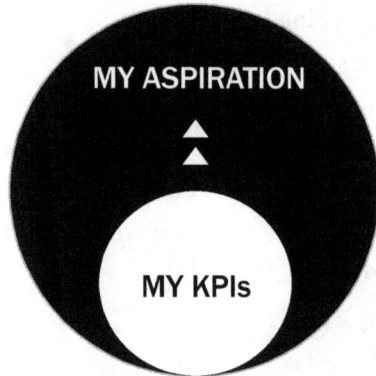

MY ASPIRATION

▲
▲

MY KPIs

**Focus on your superpower**

MY SKILLSET

▼
▼

MY SUPER-POWER

# 05 | Rule #2: Let Your Consumer Judge Your Work

In traditional work, your boss judged the quality of your work. It was simple—you had one person to answer to, the same one who assigned your responsibilities and set your performance expectations.

Today, when I ask people how many bosses they have—in other words, how many people have a say in what they do and how they do it—the answer is often at least five. There's a direct boss, a functional boss, a geography leader, and a few other important stakeholders. In technology transformations and other major change programs, this number can rise to 12 or more. With that many people weighing in, there are bound to be multiple different ideas of what great work looks like.

In a recent viral video leaked from a large financial institution, the CEO is heard raging about the fact that 14 committees are involved in a single business decision. The video may sound funny to you, but the premise is anything but.

Unsurprisingly, this dynamic undermines your sense of personal agency. There are just too many other people trying to steer what you're doing, sending you in different directions, and leaving you feeling like you have no control over any of it. When I talk to the most exhausted people, they say that after you've "pivoted" enough times, you eventually give up, stop swimming against the multiple currents, and just try to keep head above water.

It doesn't help that the bosses and stakeholders are often confused themselves. They sometimes try to assign decision rights using tools like a RACI matrix (which defines who is Responsible, Accountable, Consulted, and Informed for each task or decision in a project). One of my clients tried to make a RACI matrix for 25 decisions and 15 stakeholders; each decision ended up with at least two owners and five people checking things. By that point, there's no room for personal agency—no one can ever make a decision by themselves. In situations like that, everyone just ends up doing their best to follow the rules and avoid conflict—which is *not* the ideal way to do innovative or creative work.

What's scary is that this is being designed into organizations by consultants like me. Today's management experts believe it's the best way to tackle increasingly complex problems that require multiple specialists. It's hard to argue with that; there are usually very good reasons to involve all those stakeholders. So, executives try to align everyone by promoting teamwork and bonding. It helps a little, simply because improving communication always does. However, it doesn't last long because things change—the context evolves, new issues arise. Within a few months, the leaders are in conflict again, and the organization specialists are left confused.

How do you figure out what is true north?

The only plausible answer is the consumer—aka the audience or the user, who could be either outside or inside the organization. What matters is what's good for the person who consumes your work. That is the only possible objective standard—the only opinion that ultimately affects the success of your efforts. If the consumers think you're awesome, eventually, your bosses and stakeholders will catch on. The reverse is not true, which is why it's crucial to be disciplined and passionate about serving your consumers at every step of your work.

> If the consumers think you're awesome, eventually, your bosses and stakeholders will catch on.

## Listen to Your Consumers

Who is your consumer?

This is not a trick question. Don't complicate it—just start with the first person who uses your work.

If you're in sales, it's your buyer. If you're in HR, it's the employees you serve. If you're in procurement, it's the vendors you buy from and the employees who use what you buy. If you're in the finance department creating a report for upper management, it's the person who reads it.

In that person's eyes, what constitutes a good job on your part? Take the example of the person reading the finance report. What decisions will they make or actions will they take based on the report? Does the report make it easy for them to find and understand the information they need to make those decisions? Is it easy to access and digest within the time they have available?

Very few people ever consider questions like these. For the most part, only product developers habitually focus on the needs of their users—because their users are the customers, and the business will fail if the customers don't like the product. In other parts of the business, many people go through their entire careers and become highly successful without ever sitting down and asking the consumer what they think of the work. But in reality, the product developer mindset is critical for *everyone*, including you.

The best way to understand what your consumers want and need from you is to spend time with them. Go to them and observe how they use and respond to your work, just like a director would test-screen a movie and watch how the audience reacts in real-time. Then, sit down with them and have an in-depth conversation about it. Find out what they really care about—which might not be what you *thought* they cared about. Think creatively about what you can do to make their lives easier.

The insights you gain from this kind of first-hand observation and conversation are *much* richer than what you would get from a survey. Surveys are a popular tool for gathering feedback from customers and employees, but people usually don't fill them out thoughtfully. Responding to a survey is typically an annoying task that gets put off until the last minute, when there's no time or desire to do more than dash off a quick answer.

That's why I'm not just saying you need to get feedback from your consumers; I'm saying you need to *spend time* with them. If you're in procurement, take a vendor out to lunch. Go to the manufacturing department and see how they're using the components you procure. Go to the customer and see how those components you choose affect what they care about, like ease of cleaning, repair, and replacement.

For example, I suggested this to a long-time risk manager whose job is to point out the potential risks in a transaction. Over his 25-year career, he had attended thousands of meetings where he faced off with salespeople trying to get a transaction done, and his job—his work product—was to challenge them on the risks of the transaction. Then, he spent a few weeks attending sales meetings and observing his consumers (the salespeople) in front of their clients. He started to understand the pressure they felt and how they thought about getting deals done.

Afterward, he came back and told me that out of the 35 things he considered in his risk assessment reports, only 4 truly mattered to his consumer. What the salespeople really needed from him was to understand how the risk should influence the price, upside and downside. This man had spent his whole career feeling like he would battle with his own users—his colleagues. This new perspective changed everything.

As you gain more practice with this, you can start to broaden your perspective on who your consumer is. I told you to keep it simple and start with the most immediate people who use your work. The next step would be to look another level or two away. For example, if you're a recruiter, your immediate consumers are the candidate and the hiring manager. Look another level away, and you'll see that your work also affects the hiring manager's boss and the candidate's future teammates. What would *they* consider a job well done on your part? They might bring up considerations that your more immediate consumers didn't mention.

You'll get a lot of information from these conversations, and it might not all align perfectly. What one consumer insists is essential, another might want to completely discard. That's okay—in fact, it's inevitable. This whole exercise is about agency, not necessarily alignment. The alignment will come over time, but what's important is that the compass is in your hand. You can listen to many different people and then make your own choice about how to best serve all their needs.

For example, one of my clients has asked his team to identify the extreme users—the customers who have the *most* negative things to say about the company. Every week, he spends 3–4 hours with those users. Does it give him complete clarity? Not necessarily. They often give him wildly conflicting feedback. However, it builds goodwill, sparks insight, and keeps his attention focused on the consumer. Most importantly, it gives him agency—the ability to choose a direction and move forward confidently.

## Get Your Bosses Onboard

None of this means that your bosses and stakeholders will go away. Your performance evaluation will probably still depend on them, and you still have to meet their explicit expectations. So, it's no surprise that when I talk about this rule, I often get pushback: What if my consumers are happy with my work, but my bosses are not?

This is where the second step of this rule comes in. The first was to listen closely to your consumers and understand what they want and need from your work. The second is to transmit that message up the chain of command.

> It's up to you to make the voice of your consumers known to your bosses.

This is arguably the more challenging of the two tasks. Your superiors may not be very receptive to your message at first, especially if it contradicts their own perspective. No one likes to admit they were wrong, especially when they're in a position of authority, and *especially* not in front of their peers and rivals.

The most effective way to get your superiors to take your consumers seriously is through evidence. When you observe and interview your consumers, document their input. Record video or audio of the conversation, then analyze the transcripts for patterns across multiple consumers. What words and ideas come up most frequently? What emotions are consistently expressed? What do they consistently ask for or complain about? These factors are measurable, and clear data are a more powerful messenger than vague impressions.

Better yet, remove subjective opinion from the equation altogether if you can. Use A/B tests to see which designs, programs, or policies actually get better results in practice.

For example, one of my clients was in charge of restructuring the performance management system inside her company. In the past, the company had evaluated employees primarily based on their financial results, but the new CEO wanted to include values and behaviors in the equation as well. Every executive had an opinion, grounded in experiences with other companies or even in their personal lives. To avoid getting trapped in this whirlwind of opinions, my client had to focus on the managers and employees who would actually use the system. She developed several options and tested them with users to gather data on what kind of outcomes each would create.

This objective information cuts through the noise and helps bring the stakeholders into alignment. It's harder for them to argue with the consumers than with each other—or with you. As I mentioned before, it's a lot like screen-testing a movie. If the producers have doubts but the audience loves it, the producers will get on board.

When consulting with the consumer becomes a regular part of the entire team's process, it can have dramatically positive effects for everyone involved. For example, one of my clients in the financial sector was a large organization undergoing a major restructuring. So many parts of the company were changing, all driven from the top down, and everyone was experiencing change fatigue. People were working extra-long hours, and conflict was breaking out left and right.

To deal with this, one team decided to form a council of consumers. The change program was the work product, and the people most impacted by it were middle managers. So, the council included 30 middle managers from different departments and regions across the company. From then on, the team put every proposed change before the council.

This had a seismic impact on the ability of the organization to move forward. The council helped the team test every change and strip the program down to what was truly necessary. For the people managing the change program, life completely turned around in just a couple of months. Before the council was implemented, I had breakfast with one of them. From the look on her face when she walked in, I thought someone had died. Two months later, I had dinner with the same person, and she was smiling and laughing. I asked what had changed, and she said she had shifted her focus from the 10–12 bosses she had *thought* she was serving to the 30 consumers she *knows* she's serving.

## Stumbling Blocks

There are three big stumbling blocks that can get in the way of practicing this rule the way it's intended.

The first is failing to approach your consumer with genuine empathy. It's easy to be superficial or transactional when gathering feedback. For example, when I coach people to do this, their first instinct is to ask the consumer, "Do you like the work product?"

That's a dangerous question. You're likely to get a "yeah, sure" kind of response, then pat yourself on the back and go back to work—but you haven't really learned anything. You didn't get any insight about the daily life of the consumer, and they didn't really open up to you about their true desires, needs, or complaints. Why? Because you didn't take the time to show a genuine interest in them.

The truth is, most people rarely receive focused attention from *anyone* for more than a moment. They rarely get the opportunity to express themselves uninterrupted to someone who is actually *listening*. If you give them that—if you show that you truly care about their perspective and are willing to hear them out fully—they will open up to you. But if you do what most people do—ask a few shallow, self-serving questions and half-listen to the answers—they will brush you off.

Another stumbling block could be your own desire for support and validation from your superiors. Let's say you have some bosses who are really nice to you and look out for you. It's natural to be swayed by their opinions and overlook the perspective of others, including the consumer.

That's dangerous in modern work—dangerous both for the quality of your work and for your career. If you're not in direct contact with consumers regularly, you might not even realize that their assessment of your work doesn't align with your boss's view. Constantly seeking for the approval of that kind boss is not a path to agency—it's a path to dependency. You're giving the steering wheel to someone else, and they might not always be right.

One final potential problem is a boss or stakeholder who is actively going against the best interests of the consumer and the organization. Personally, I believe it's always better to know for sure than to fool yourself, hope, and pray. So, make an effort to spend time with your consumers and get your superiors on board with the consumers' needs. If you find that they simply don't care, you have a decision to make:

leave, change teams, or keep trying. Many people in this situation choose to stay because, even when their stakeholders continue to grumble and pull them in different directions, they find great satisfaction in focusing on the consumer, knowing they're truly serving the person who matters.

## Conclusion

At its core, this rule is simply about moving your attention from one conversation (with your boss) to another (with your consumer). It's one of the most liberating things you can do for yourself because it marks a significant shift from dependency to genuine freedom.

This is true even for senior leaders. I see plenty of executives who have never really practiced this. They were trained early in their careers to focus on pleasing their superiors, and they climbed the ladder by successfully managing upward. Then, when they reach the C-suite, they end up making decisions based on politics rather than what's truly best for the people who are impacted.

Regardless of your level or challenges in the organization, this rule can dramatically change how you feel about your work. When you feel forced to pursue objectives you think are pointless, misguided, conflicting, or nonsensical, it takes all the wind out of your sails. You feel frustrated, confused, and unmotivated—and understandably so. Focusing on the consumer counteracts this; it creates a powerful sense of clarity and purpose, showing you exactly how your work can make a positive difference for someone else.

This rule, however, is challenging to follow in Asian cultures because of the premium we often place on human loyalty. I advise my

Asian clients to think about refining and adjusting the definition of loyalty. True loyalty is not about blindly following instructions. It is about orientation. Taking time to orient your stakeholder to what will matter for their success, and being respectful and patient during the journey to get there.

# VISUAL SUMMARY : LET YOUR CONSUMER JUDGE YOUR WORK

WHEN YOUR
CONSUMER JUDGES
YOUR WORK HIGHLY
...

"I WILL RECOMMEND YOUR WORK TO OTHERS"

"YOUR WORK HELPED ME SUCCEED"

"I WILL ALWAYS COME TO YOU FOR SIMILAR WORK"

... YOUR BOSS(ES)
WILL JUDGE YOU
POSITIVELY

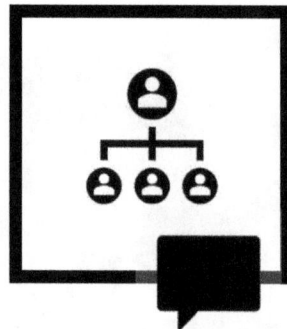

"YOU ARE HIGHLY PRODUCTIVE"

"YOUR EXPERTISE IS VALUED"

"OTHERS LIKE TO WORK WITH YOU"

# 06 Rule #3: Focus on Aspirations (Future) and Actions (Now)

Although the ten rules in this book can be implemented in any order, there is a logical flow when cultivating personal agency. First, you need to figure out who you are and where you're going—that's what Rule #1 is about. Then, you need to align your compass, or your motivation from Rule #1 will start to fade—that's what Rule #2 is for. The next logical step is to set clear goals.

Most companies set a certain amount of goals for you. They have yearly strategic plans that cascade down to quarterly goals, which translate into specific KPIs for you. Studies have shown that more than half of all employees fail to meet these targets; actually hitting KPIs (never mind exceeding them) is the exception rather than the rule (Gartner, 2023). And when you're behind, you meet with your boss, and they tell you that you need to catch up.

I call this the "Are we there yet?" conversation. There's this idea that a high performance organization has these conversations more frequently, more seriously, with tougher consequences: if you don't meet your goals, you'll pay the price. But as we established in Rule #1, that kind of external "motivation" doesn't generate high performance. Quite the opposite; it's one of the most surefire ways to *reduce* personal agency, and therefore, *undermine* performance. In fact, when I talk to people with very low agency and ask about their goals, they invariably tell me their quarterly targets.

---

The answer is not to do away with goals but
to change the time horizon of goals.

---

The problem isn't just that the goals are set by someone else and driven by external punishments and rewards. It's that the time frame is neither here nor there. Long-term goals (measured in years) are aspirational; they inspire you with a grand vision and are closely tied to your purpose. They release a hormone in your brain, serotonin, that is often referred to as the 'feel good' hormone. The right set of long-term aspirations will remind you why you are taking on the frustrations and pressures of everyday work and keep you motivated even through your darkest days.

Short-term goals (measured in days) are actionable; they give you a sense of concrete accomplishment. They release a different hormone in your brain, dopamine, that is often referred to as the 'reward and pleasure' hormone. Setting clear short-term goals in the form of tasks that you can complete will give you a sense of achievement and progress every day, and keep you motivated to get up and go again.

Medium-term goals (measured in months) aren't big enough to inspire you, and you can't cross them off your to-do list, so all you can do is worry about them. They produce the 'stress' hormone, cortisol. They are based on assumptions, not on aspiration or action. When it comes to goal setting, that time frame is, quite literally, the zone of anxiety.

So, how do you set goals in a way that strengthens your personal agency instead of undermining it? Focus on aspirations and 'actions, not assumptions. Choose your long-term ambitions, then create daily and weekly habits that consistently move you in that direction, one concrete step at a time.

## Two Kinds of Goals

One of the biggest factors contributing to burnout is constant pressure to keep up with rapid change and meet other people's expectations. That's one of the reasons why extra vacation days and free yoga classes don't help much. Even when you're not actively working, that pressure is still hanging over your head. There's no use in telling people to just take a break and trust that things will fall into place—they won't. The need to hustle is very real.

However, hustle *can* be invigorating instead of draining.

There's a difference between pressure, which
is imposed from the outside and saps
your energy, and intensity.

Intensity comes from within, from a desire to give your best effort and accomplish something that matters. To understand what I mean, think of an elite sports team. Every player brings their own intensity to every practice and every game because they *want* to win. They *want* to be the best. They're hustling, but it's sustainable in the long term because the hustle is driven by intensity from the inside, not pressure from the outside.

To create that intensity, you must have the right kind of goals: aspirations and actions.

Let's start with the aspirations—the long-term goals. When I say long-term, I mean *very* long. I like to use a horizon of 3 years; anything less than two, and you risk dipping into the zone of anxiety.

It's important to think that far into the future because your long-term goals should be *big*. In fact, it's better not to think of them as goals but as dreams with numbers. This is not the time to worry about practicality or achievability. Instead, envision yourself 2–5 years into the future. What would you *love* to have achieved in your professional life by then? What would make you feel like you had done something truly worthwhile?

For an athlete, it might be winning the league championship. For a writer, it might be writing a bestseller. For an executive, it might be doubling the size of the business. Whatever it is for you, it should be clearly linked to the sense of purpose you got from Rule #1. Purpose alone isn't enough; you need something specific to aim for, or you won't feel like you're truly taking hold of the steering wheel in your work life.

Once your aspirations are clear, move your focus to a 1–2 week horizon. What can you do *immediately* to make progress toward your long-term goals, even if that progress is just baby steps? If you work backward from the end point you're envisioning to where you're starting now, what should you start doing today? I call this "habit-setting" instead of goal-setting, because the intention is to create habits of action that you perform consistently, on a weekly or daily basis.

For example, let's say my goal is to double the size of my business in the next 3 years. To do that, I need to grow and strengthen both my client base and my team. Here are some of the habitual actions I take to support that aim:

- Having lunch with clients at least twice a week
- Traveling to at least two cities a week
- Meeting with a regional team at least once a week
- Having four to five coaching calls a day with members of my team

If you're not entirely sure what habits will lead to your aspirations, start with your best guess, then re-evaluate every 3 months or so. The most important thing is to take action—to not do *nothing*. When you're unsure of what to do, it's tempting to just stay still until you figure it out, but you won't gain any new information by holding still. Start taking *some* steps forward, even if they're not exactly on the right path; you'll encounter things along the way that will guide you which way to go.

The most effective people put these habits into their calendars, embedding them into their day-to-day routines to make sure they actually get done. This particular list is all work-related tasks, but your habits can also include personal tasks if they help you make progress toward your aspirations. For example, if your aspirations require you to be a better leader, your habit might include daily meditation, reading, or other self-development activities.

Every time you complete one of these tasks, you get a dopamine hit. It actually *feels* rewarding, precisely *because* there's a strong connection between the aspirations and the habits. This is what allows you to feel a high level of agency, even when your long-term goals are extremely difficult and distant, and it keeps the intensity from becoming exhausting.

Think about those elite athletes again. Winning a championship is a tall order; in any given league, many teams go decades without that victory. But showing up to your scheduled workout and giving your maximum effort to every repetition and every drill—that's totally doable. And when they do it, they *know* they're taking a crucial step toward that championship, even if it's still far away.

## Look Beyond the Status Quo

The people who struggle the most with Rule #3 are the ones who haven't really thought through Rules #1 and #2. If you don't have a clear understanding of your own purpose and the impact of your work on others, it's hard to articulate any aspirations beyond maintaining the status quo. In my experience, people who work in back-office functions are the most likely to find themselves drawing a blank here.

For example, I recently worked with a group of recruiters. When I asked about their goals for the next 2 or 3 years, they had no idea beyond simply keeping their jobs or getting a promotion. They hadn't thought deeply about what they were trying to do for the candidates and hiring managers they served. So, they had daily routines—screen 50 resumes, conduct 10 interviews—but those actions weren't energizing because they weren't linked to any meaningful long-term aspirations.

If you think back-office jobs don't lend themselves to this rule, think about administrative assistants—a classic back-office role. I've worked with assistants who were absolute rock stars with massive personal agency. Think Donna from the TV legal drama *Suits*—always ten steps ahead of everyone, going above and beyond the call of duty, and taking immense pride and satisfaction in her work.

Why does Donna have so much personal agency? Because she is focused on the consumers of her work: her boss and his clients. She is completely in touch with their needs and desires, which gives her a genuine sense of motivation and aspiration. That, in turn, feeds a rhythm and intensity in her daily work.

That's very different from an assistant who has no long-term goal beyond completing her tasks day in and day out. A person like that might have very strong habits and routines, but the intensity, drive, and sparkle would be missing. Those routines, instead of being small steps that build toward something worthwhile, would simply be repetitive, boring work—which is the opposite of what we're trying to create here.

## Aim Extra-High

When I first started practicing this rule with my team, I worried that if we stopped thinking about our quarterly numbers, we would fall behind our targets.

The same is almost certainly true for you. Just because you start focusing on your aspirations and habits doesn't mean your company will stop setting quarterly goals for you. I know you can't change that. You don't have to. You just need to make sure you do two things right.

The first is to ensure that your long-term aspirations are aligned with your company's medium-term expectations of you. You need to be able to meet those expectations *on the way* to your long-term goals. If your aspirations pull you in a different direction than where your company wants you to go, you'll obviously run into trouble.

The second is to set your habits to exceed your company's expectations. For example, if the firm wants me to do $20 million in business next year, I set my personal bar at $30—35 million and use *that* figure to calibrate my habits. In other words, I intentionally aim to over-achieve. This allows me to trust that my daily and weekly habits will lead me to my goals each quarter, without having to actively track or worry about those medium-term goals.

This might sound a little crazy, but it really works in practice. I have about 100 people on my team. If my firm is expecting X from us, my personal goal is 2X. But if you add up what my team actually does, it ends up being 6X.

The amazing thing is that this happens without me having to crack the whip *at all*. In traditional work, managers set stretch goals; each team member sets their own goals, and then the manager asks for more. My team does the opposite. My team members set crazy goals for themselves because they *want* to—they're motivated and driven—and I actually have to pull them back a little to keep them from overextending themselves.

## From Random to Rhythm

When I talk to low-agency people about how they feel at work, a certain sensation comes up repeatedly. They feel tossed around, pulled all over the place, and forever uncertain about what to do or what's coming at them next. I call this the washing machine. It's random motion—no structure, no predictability, no direction—and it's the lived experience of the vast majority of white-collar workers today.

One of the greatest benefits of Rule #3 is that it gets you out of the washing machine. Your habits create routines for you. They introduce structure, predictability and, most importantly, rhythm. This allows you to do something extremely powerful: see your work day as an enjoyable dance.

> They introduce structure, predictability and, most importantly, rhythm. This allows you to do something extremely powerful: see your work day as an enjoyable dance.

All dance is about moves executed one at a time, carefully, in an orchestrated manner. To truly enjoy your work, you have to transition from randomness to rhythm.

You probably know about the dangers of multitasking. Your brain takes time to adjust between different tasks, so every time you stop doing one thing and start doing another—even if it's just pausing to glance at your phone or answer a quick email—you lose a little time and focus. The momentum you had with the first task dissipates, and now you have to get it started again.

We've all heard that single-tasking is more efficient and productive than multitasking, but most people don't actually practice it. I used to be one of the worst offenders. I thought you had to be a highly disciplined person to work that way, and I'm terribly *undisciplined* by nature—I like creativity, variety, and spontaneity.

However, I no longer see discipline as a trait you either have or don't have. It's an *outcome*. The real reason most people can't focus on one thing at a time isn't because they lack some internal power to do so. It's because they don't know which thing to focus on at any given moment.

Having clear, repeatable habits on a daily or weekly basis goes a long way toward solving this problem. I've witnessed it first-hand, both for myself and my team. The act of setting my routine is what brings discipline into my life. I don't have to become disciplined first. In other words, you don't *think* yourself into doing this; you *do* yourself into thinking this.

And when you do, it *feels* good. You get to experience flow—that state of mind where your attention is so deep, and your progress is so steady, that you actually lose track of time. You save yourself from the stress of deciding what to do at every moment of every day. Most importantly, you get more done, and every time you complete a task, you get a little hit of dopamine. This adds up to higher motivation day after day, week after week.

At the same time, having clear aspirations and habits makes it much easier to know what *not* to do. Especially if you're in a leadership position, you probably receive constant requests for your time, and not all of them serve your goals. Do you really need to attend that meeting, give that talk, sit on that committee, or go on that business trip? Check your short- and long-term goals. If you don't see a clear fit, protect your time and energy, and just say no.

That said, sometimes there are good distractions—opportunities to meet someone or explore something new and interesting. If every day is packed to the gills with rigidly scheduled tasks, there's no room for that kind of serendipity. So, I intentionally mark out space in my calendar for the unexpected. If something comes up that piques my interest, I have pre-blocked time to dig into it.

In summary, find the underlying rhythm to your work using carefully thought- through repeatable habits that line your calendar. But create enough free space to explore serendipity.


## Conclusion

Rule #3 was one of the first rules I applied for myself and my team, and what it has done for us is nothing short of life-changing. We track our progress weekly based on the goals we've set for ourselves, and for the last 3 years, we've been well ahead of the expectations of the rest of the firm.

As a team leader, my role has completely changed. Instead of worrying about driving productivity, I get to focus on nurturing my team members and preserving them as assets. Their level of intensity has skyrocketed, without any pushing on my part. Plus, all my anxiety and obsession around meeting quarterly targets have disappeared. A while ago, a colleague asked me in the elevator, "How's your quarter going?" I didn't know—it took me a moment to even remember what month it was.

For individual practitioners, this rule creates a much stronger sense of control and self-worth at work. When you focus on medium-term goals, you spend your days wondering how to reach them, getting pulled in a hundred directions, and making moment-to-moment decisions about how best to use your time. Refocusing your attention on long-term aspirations and short-term habits injects purpose, rhythm, and balance into your work life. Your calendar is full of purposeful tasks, so you know what to do and can focus on one task at a time. This helps you get into a flow and accomplish more, which means more dopamine hits and higher motivation. And when your calendar is packed with these productive, habitual tasks, it's no longer open for others to fill. You're in control.

The key to making this rule work is to be the author of your own aspirations and habits. They must come from a genuine, authentic place; otherwise, you will end up resenting them as much as you resent the quarterly KPIs handed down to you. That's why it's the third rule, not the first. If you do the work on Rules #1 and #2, they will set you up for success with Rule #3, putting you well on your way to achieving high personal agency.

# VISUAL SUMMARY : FOCUS ON ASPIRATIONS AND ACTIONS

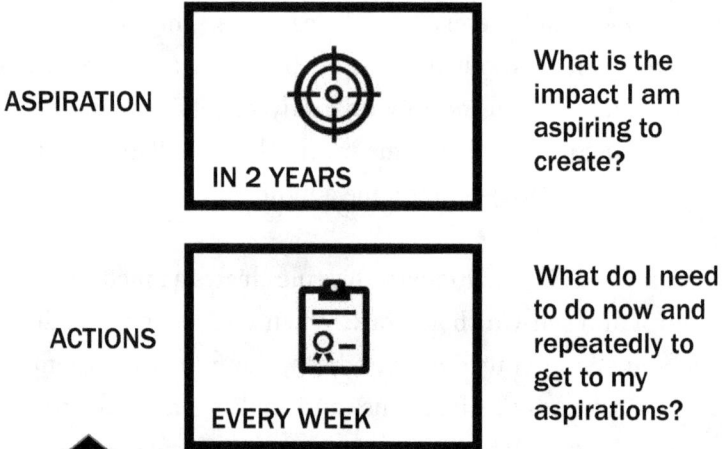

ASPIRATION

IN 2 YEARS

What is the impact I am aspiring to create?

ACTIONS

EVERY WEEK

What do I need to do now and repeatedly to get to my aspirations?

If you do this well ....

... achieving this feels easy

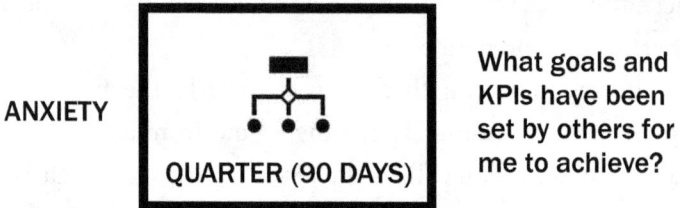

ANXIETY

QUARTER (90 DAYS)

What goals and KPIs have been set by others for me to achieve?

# 07 | Rule #4: Press Refresh Every Week

U ntil a few years ago, I used to hold a monthly call with my team to bring everyone together and establish priorities for the coming month. We would spend an hour or more hashing everything out, carefully planning and assigning tasks. Then, reality would set it. By the middle of the first week, all our carefully laid plans would invariably fall apart.

My anxiety was building up, and I was losing my sense of personal agency. Every night, I'd go to bed worried, and every day, I'd come to work frantic. I would pick up the phone and check on people and projects randomly, hoping it would help to keep everything on track. Of course, all it did was transmit my anxiety to everyone else on the team.

Between 1 monthly call and the next, there was no mechanism to re-establish my sense of agency—or anyone else's. Inevitably, each call turned into a post-mortem discussion about who was to blame for the problems that arose the previous month. Our team calls became something no one looked forward to. What was supposed to be a mechanism to rebuild ourselves had become its opposite—an energy drain instead of an energy source.

I was looking for a way to fix those calls, and someone suggested that for our next call, we should skip the business discussion and just check in on everyone's mental state. It was early in the pandemic, and everyone was struggling with lockdown, fear, and grief over loved ones who had fallen ill or passed away. I agreed, and it turned out to be exceptionally helpful. My team opened up about how overwhelmed they were and the challenges they were facing, and everyone was supportive.

It felt good, but it didn't quite solve the problem. We hadn't discussed our business priorities, and we needed to. There had to be a way to do both.

One colleague suggested that instead of meeting monthly, we meet weekly, with a very simple agenda consisting of three questions:

- What did I win last week?
- What did I learn last week?
- What am I planning to win this week?

We tried it for a few weeks and found that as long as we stuck to this simple agenda, each person could cover what was important to discuss in about 5 minutes. The format allowed us to address business priorities and mental states at the same time. It was like a quick refresh that brought everyone **back into alignment**, kept us on track, or helped us adjust our course if necessary.

> In effect, we had created the simplest mechanism to allow each member of the team to refresh their personal agency every 7 days.

I began to see that having a regular refresh on a short time horizon—one week, or two at most—was crucial for re-establishing agency, meaning, and well-being for myself and my team. Since then, this simple weekly session has replaced a huge amount of tedious planning and coordination.

No doubt, you have experienced something like what my team used to go through. You plan everything out perfectly, then Monday morning comes, and you're hit with urgent requests, upset clients, unexpected crises, upended priorities, and all sorts of other disruptions. Everything gets thrown completely off track, and that's a huge blow to your sense of personal agency. It feels like the steering wheel has been yanked out of your hand. What you need is a way to re-establish your personal agency when things go haywire—a process to address what's urgent and then get back on track.

The solution is simple: set a 1- to 2-week horizon and choose one thing to focus on accomplishing. Then, at the end of that period, you assess what went well, what you've learned, and how you'll move forward. This simple process will replenish your energy, focus your attention, and re-establish your personal agency.

## Wins, Learnings, and Plans

The idea of a work sprint comes from the world of Agile software development. To put it simply, the team creates a plan for a short time horizon, often referred to as a sprint (traditionally 2 weeks), executes it, then pauses reflect and adjust before moving forward. The short horizon is crucial because things change rapidly. The business environment, priorities, resources, information available, stakeholder needs—these things might be totally different 2 weeks down the road, and you'll have to change course.

The best way to manage this is through a simple conversation focused on three things: wins, learnings, and plans.

## Wins

Wins are the accomplishments of the team. What got done? What went well? What are you proud of? What should be celebrated?

For example, maybe you (or your team) closed a deal, averted a crisis, hired a new team member, nailed a client presentation, organized a successful event, preserved a clean safety record, or secured the funding you've been asking. Obviously, the nature of your wins will depend on the kind of work you do.

> Whatever is meaningful to you and
> your team, say it out loud.

If you're not in the habit of acknowledging wins, it might seem like a silly practice. Do we really need to pat ourselves on the back for doing our jobs? To put it bluntly, yes! The human brain is heavily biased toward the negative; we're hardwired to pay about twice as much attention to obstacles, threats, and other bad things as we do to positive things. So, if you don't explicitly recognize your achievements, your brain will fixate on your problems and failures.

That is not a helpful state of mind. It saps your motivation and sense of agency, making it harder to stay focused and productive. How you feel emotionally *matters*, and the last thing you want to do is slip into a downward spiral of worry and self-criticism. Taking a moment to celebrate your wins helps keep you in a positive, empowered frame of mind.

## Learnings

Learnings are lessons you can carry forward from the challenges you faced over the past week. What new solutions did you create? What new tools did you discover? How can you do things a little better next time? How can you avoid facing the same challenges again?

For example, maybe you found a way to automate a task you used to do manually. Perhaps you refined your interview process to hire candidates who are a better fit. Maybe you discovered a weak point in your supply chain that needs to be addressed. Again, the specifics will depend on your context, but I encourage you to think broadly—include both the small and big stuff. Yes, even if it's just a little trick that shaves a few minutes off a repetitive task.

The key here is to stay focused on the future, not the past. This is not a run-down of everything that went wrong in the past week, and it's definitely not an opportunity to assign blame for those things. It's a chance to share information that will help everyone improve going forward.

This part of the conversation is an extremely powerful driver of team performance. While there's the obvious benefit of preventing future problems and improving efficiency, there's also a more subtle and even more profound impact. When everyone is invited to offer suggestions for improvement, their sense of agency increases. They feel respected and valued as team members, they feel a greater sense of ownership over their work, and they feel empowered to think critically and creatively about it.

## Plans

Plans are your intentions for the coming week. How has your environment changed since the previous meeting? What is your top priority now? What must get done before your next meeting, and how will you measure success?

For example, maybe a big project has gone off track and you need to get in back on course. Maybe you need to get ballooning costs under control. Maybe you need to fix a critical software bug. Or perhaps you need to pivot the messaging in your marketing campaign. This is your chance to assess your current situation, set a fresh agenda, and start the week with renewed clarity.

In this part of the conversation, it's crucial to stay tightly focused. The goal here is not to lay out your entire to-do list, which is probably a mile long and completely overwhelming. Instead, it's to figure out what is the *one* thing that's most important to accomplish. Unless you force yourself to establish clear priorities and stick to them, you'll end up trying to do too many things at once and accomplishing none of them.

Realistically, even with this narrow focus, there's a good chance you'll get pulled in many different directions in the coming week. As I mentioned at the beginning of this chapter, even the best-laid plans often get tossed in the washing machine on Monday morning. But if you don't have clear priorities, that washing machine will be far more disorienting and destructive than if you have something solid to anchor yourself to.

So that's it: wins, learnings, and plans. That's the whole conversation—simple, brief, and remarkably effective.

At an individual level, you can even do this every day. Start your day with 5 or 10 minutes to lay all this out for yourself, or do it at the end of the day so you can hit the ground running the next morning. This is not a revolutionary practice; you can even buy planners and journals that include these questions on every page.

However, the real power lies in having this conversation collectively with your team. In modern work, the level of interdependence is so high. Each person doing this individually will not create the alignment needed for the team to function well. The more you rely on others' work to enable your own work, the more important it is to do this together.

This is especially true for junior employees, whose baseline level of agency is typically lower. They lack years of experience to give them confidence in deciding what's important or improving how things are done. In my experience, these conversations are one of the keys to help them get comfortable in their roles, establish a sense of belonging, and start showing the true extent of their talents.

In the end, this weekly refresh isn't really about prioritizing your tasks and organizing your calendar. It's about tricking your brain into not feeling anxious. Things will still come up that force you to adjust or even abandon your plans in the middle of the week, but you won't stress about it as much because you'll know that in a few days, you'll have a chance to reset.

## Five Reasons to Refresh, not Review

In most organizations, any backward-looking meeting—like a review or post-mortem—is usually a downer. The natural tendency is to focus on what went wrong and who is to blame. Even when the team just had a big win, it doesn't take long for everyone's attention to shift toward the challenges ahead. People dread these meetings; as soon as they give their report, they disengage mentally. This whole dynamic creates a very real and problematic drain on everyone's energy.

However, a good refresh meeting should actually *boost* the team's energy, not drain it. This happens in five different ways.

## (1) Recognizing wins

No matter who you are or what your job is, there are probably at least three or four moments every week that give you a sense of winning. A win could be related to actual business results, like finishing a project or winning a deal. It could be something you've learned, like a new tool that makes an annoying task much easier. Or it could be an emotional victory, like having an unexpectedly productive conversation with a difficult colleague.

Recounting those wins (big or small) in public every week creates a huge energy boost. If you're used to evaluating your achievements over longer time horizons—as most white-collar workers are—you'll find that shifting to shorter time blocks is immensely satisfying. It feels much better to get 90 percent of the way to your 1-week goal than just 2 percent of the way to your annual goal. When you can point to a concrete step you've taken, even if it's a baby step, it gives you the energy to keep moving forward.

The simple act of celebrating a few wins and learnings—even when other things aren't going according to plan—helps turn your attention to the progress you've made instead of worrying about everything still left to do. Recognizing that progress keeps anxiety at bay by giving you a sense of meaning and self-efficacy.

## (2) Learning from setbacks

Failures, losses, and mistakes are inevitable. Naturally, they can be upsetting, sometimes devastating. For example, let's say you've built a great relationship with a potential client and have been talking about a possible deal for months. It seemed like a sure thing—you even reached a verbal agreement—but at the last minute, they pulled out and gave the deal to someone else. It feels like a sucker punch—not just a commercial setback but an emotional one.

You can wallow in that negative energy... or you and your team can transform it into something positive. How? By detaching emotionally, suspending all judgment, and analyzing the event like a specimen in a lab.

- *What are the motivations of this person in this context?*
- *What are all the factors that contributed to this outcome?*
- *Next time we find ourselves in a similar situation, what are the warning signals we should look out for?*

When you do this with a supportive team, the negative energy of the setback quickly transforms into the positive energy of learning.

## (3) Regaining control

One of the top reasons people feel so burnt out is because business is evolving faster and becoming more complex at a rate we've never experienced before. It's not your fault as an individual—you haven't become less competent or resilient. It's just that the rapid pace of change makes it exceedingly difficult to maintain your balance. The practice of regular refresh allows you to regain that balance frequently, so you never stay off-kilter or out of control for too long.

The sweet spot for re-prioritization depends on your role. As I mentioned earlier, at an individual level, it can be useful to do this every day. Mid-level managers should re-prioritize with their teams every week. For senior leaders, this horizon can be longer—maybe every month.

Again, re-prioritizing isn't necessarily about ranking all the activities you plan to do. The goal is to allocate your attention and energy on a few specific things. In other words, what would it take to win your day, week, or month? What key things do you need to accomplish to call it a victory? It should be a small number of things so your brain can focus its attention on them. By making that decision internally for yourself (and your team), your brain will help you follow through.

This practice helps you take ownership of the inevitable reality of re-prioritization. Priorities will change frequently, no matter what you do. When you feel like it's happening *to* you, it's frustrating and anxiety-inducing. However, when it's an expected part of your routine, it feels like you're in control, and it energizes you instead of draining you.

## (4) Being focused

One of my favorite effects of the refresh process is that it makes me comfortable with saying no to things that are not aligned with my priorities for the week. Everyone advises saying no to things that don't matter. But in reality—especially for junior employees—it's often hard to find the courage to say no. Even for a senior partner like me, it can be extremely hard to say no to client requests.

However, we all know that being selective with our energy and attention is essential to avoiding burnout. Burnout is a function of open decisions—all the things you haven't decided on, acted upon, or closed. Even if you take time off work, even while you're asleep, those "open items" are lingering at the back of your mind. The only way to truly recharge and reboot is by closing those open items. The re-prioritization aspect of this process helps you make firm decisions, so things feel closed. That's why it's good to do this at the end of the week, so you can go home for the weekend feeling at peace with the previous week and prepared for the next one.

## (5) Staying connected

We are social creatures—it's an inescapable fact of the human condition. It feels good to share our stories and hear the stories of others. It feels even better to help others and receive their help in return. When we connect in these ways, we gain energy.

That's why it's so important to press refresh *with your team*. Of course, if that's not an option, you can still do this process individually and get huge benefits from it. However, the full power of this practice is inextricably tied to the relationships that grow from it. If you're not in charge of your team, I challenge you to at least introduce the idea of weekly recalibration to your team leader. See if they're open to trying it; the benefits are well worth the effort for everyone involved.

## How to Press Refresh Right

When I see individuals and teams struggling to implement this and reap its full benefits, it's usually due to one—or sometimes both— of two reasons.

### (1) Putting it off

This refresh process is only truly effective when it becomes a habit. To get all the benefits, you have to do it every single week, without fail. This kind of consistency is only possible if you treat this process as an essential, non-negotiable task.

It's easy to *not* do that, especially when you're already feeling overwhelmed and short on time. In those circumstances, stopping to reflect on your day or your week feels like a luxury—or maybe even a waste of time. Even with the best intentions, urgent things can get in the way. You tell yourself you'll do it once the urgent task is done, but Friday evening arrives and you just want to get to the weekend. Then Monday morning comes with its chaos, and the refresh simply never happens.

## (2) Ignoring the emotions

If you recall from the beginning of this chapter, for my team, this refresh process started as a mental health check-in during a particularly stressful time. That emotional reboot is central to the purpose of this rule. Sometimes, teams come together to assess their work but gloss over or ignore the emotional aspect, turning it into nothing more than a task organization meeting (which probably doesn't need to be a team meeting at all). This is especially common in cultures where emotional openness is generally discouraged, such as in East Asia.

I know many people who are meticulous about planning their week—some even block out time on their calendar for doing nothing or going for a walk, which certainly helps. However, they're still missing that team-wide emotional reboot. It does involve some vulnerability, so it might feel uncomfortable at first. But remember, the primary purpose of this rule is not to organize your tasks but to maintain a healthy state of mind. If you deny yourself the chance to celebrate wins, recognize learnings, and address concerns, you miss the chance to refresh your mental energy and motivation. In my experience, if you go 3 weeks in a row without a refresh in an emotionally open and honest way, you will start to lose momentum.

## Conclusion

A few years ago, one of my team members was running two large projects at the same time. She constantly complained about feeling overwhelmed.

I talked to her recently, and she was now running six programs simultaneously—and feeling totally comfortable. It's not that her core skill of prioritization has improved threefold. It's because, thanks to this rule, her brain has stopped overheating. Regular refresh enables her to process lots of information, organize them, and act on them calmly, even when unexpected events take things in a new direction.

It also helps her say no when she needs to. She used to be the first to volunteer for anything her colleagues needed help with, even when she was already overloaded. A few weeks ago, she said one of her wins was saying no to a research project I was working on. She was able to make that decision with confidence and celebrate it publicly because she now has a level of clarity and focus she never had before.

With that, let's take a moment to look back on the four rules of personal agency:

1. Bring your own motivation.
2. Let your consumer judge your work.
3. Focus on aspirations and actions.
4. Press refresh every week.

Although you don't have to master these rules in this exact order, there's a natural flow here. First, you figure out what's driving you—your personal purpose at work. Then, you find your north star—the most reliable, meaningful measure of a job well done. After that, you set long-term goals to inspire you and short-term goals to make concrete progress. Finally, you take time every week to assess your current situation, recognize your achievements, and pivot if necessary. These four actions create a powerful sense of ownership and control over your life at work, regardless of your role, your boss, your company policies, or any other external factors.

Notice that none of this is about taking a break or disconnecting from work. Rest is vital for staying physically and mentally healthy—I would never deny that. However, it's not the answer to burnout. Even taking a whole month off work solves nothing if you return to the same situation you left: a washing machine that leaves you feeling overwhelmed and out of control.

In the long run, the only sustainable solution to burnout is putting yourself in the driver's seat of your work life every day, and these four rules show you how.

# VISUAL SUMMARY : PRESS REFRESH EVERY WEEK

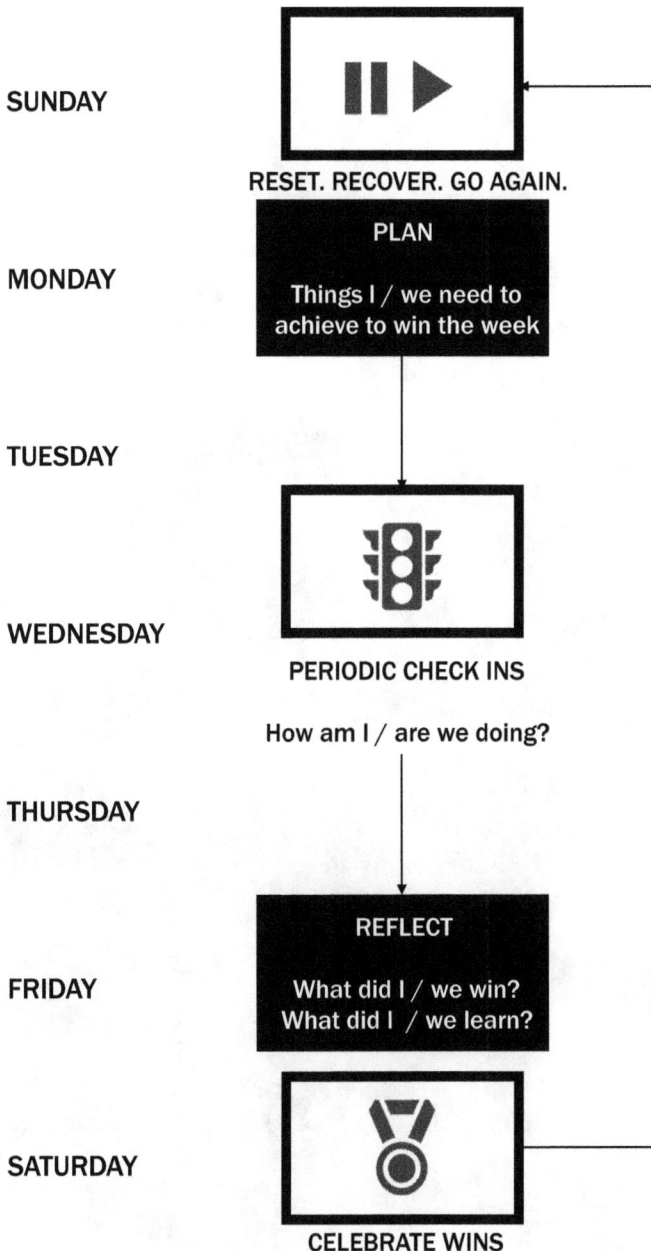

**SUNDAY**

⏸ ▶

RESET. RECOVER. GO AGAIN.

**MONDAY**

PLAN

Things I / we need to achieve to win the week

**TUESDAY**

**WEDNESDAY**

PERIODIC CHECK INS

How am I / are we doing?

**THURSDAY**

**FRIDAY**

REFLECT

What did I / we win?
What did I / we learn?

**SATURDAY**

CELEBRATE WINS

# PART III
## SOCIAL AGENCY

"It is easy to work with people who think like you. Social agency is the ability to collaborate with people who you just 'don't get'."

Up to this point, our focus has been on developing **personal agency**: your ability to take ownership and control over your daily life at work. That takes you a long way on the spectrum from burning out to thriving, but it's not enough by itself. Even if you do a great job of managing your own time, energy, and mental state, other people will have a huge impact on your overall level of agency. Your interactions with them can be sources of overwhelm, frustration, and anxiety...

---

... or they can be sources of energy,
motivation, and power.

---

That's what **social agency** is about: participating in the agency of others and helping them participate in yours.

This means far more than just having collegial relationships or a group of friends at work. Each person in your work community has their own agency, and your agency is connected to theirs. When those connections are weak, it's like a brain where all the neurons are isolated; there's massive potential, but it's trapped. In this modern world of highly interdependent work, you can't accomplish anything of significance by yourself. That's why it's so important to intentionally strengthen the connections between your agency and the agency of the people around you.

This doesn't happen by accident. In most offices, the default relationship is transactional. You probably know a little about your colleagues personally, but most of your interactions are about what they can do for you. You look at them as resources, not sources of agency, and they view you the same way.

This has only become truer over time. As I've mentioned before, the average time in a role is 4–5 years for Gen X, 2–3 years for Millennials, and only about 7 months for Gen Z. Compare this with my parents' generation, when it wasn't unusual for a person to spend a decade or more in the same office, embedded in the same web of relationships. Back then, it was common to have very close relationships at work, sometimes even closer than family.

Now, workplace mobility is so high that most people develop only weak ties to their colleagues, if any at all. Plus, it takes an investment of time and energy to deepen work relationships beyond the transactional, and the current levels of burnout mean that people often just want to go home at the end of the day. They have no energy left for relationship building. Our innate need to connect and be socially rooted to a community is as strong as ever, but that need is much less likely to be fulfilled in a work context today than 20 years ago.

That said, let me ask you this: if you're feeling overwhelmed at work, would it be better to be isolated from everyone else and deal with it alone, or to have support from the people around you? Of course, it would be better to have support.

Now flip that around: if you have high agency and are highly motivated at work, would you rather have people around you who sap and undermine that energy, or who support and feed it? Obviously, the latter.

As we shift our focus to social agency, you'll see that the full picture of agency is about more than being in the driver's seat of your life. It's also about having an impact on the world—making a difference to and for other people. Think about this in terms of both giving and receiving. You can have a positive impact on others by giving them your time, energy, and skills. You can also amplify your positive impact on the world by leveraging the time, energy, and skills of others. High-quality social connections create benefits in both directions, whether you're the one giving or the one receiving. It's a win both ways.

This isn't the transactional exchange of resources and favors that we're familiar with in the workplace. It's not quid pro quo, where you do something for someone and then expect them to help you out in return. It's symbiosis—the very act of helping someone else actually boosts your energy and agency, independent of anything they might do for you in return. The same is true when you're on the receiving end. It's truly a mutually beneficial relationship.

For so many people, interactions at work are a source of friction that makes everything slower and more difficult. You're forever struggling to get what you want and need from others, negotiating complicated power dynamics, and maneuvering to get closer to people with more influence and resources. It's exhausting.

The rules of social agency help you turn that dynamic on its head. As you start to practice them, a significant amount of that friction will disappear, and some of it will turn into fuel that helps you achieve your goals. You'll see that when you participate in other people's agency and let them participate in yours, there's a multiplier effect on both sides, and life suddenly gets a lot easier.

"When you actively participate in other people's agency, they will want to actively participate in yours... you'll begin to see help, support, and collaboration— green lights instead of red."

# 08 | Rule #5: Expand Your Relationship Radius

A while back, I had a one-on-one meeting with a client. We only had 45 minutes together, and I had a list of 16 important strategy questions I needed answers to. I even brought a junior consultant with me to take notes.

However, instead of launching immediately into my agenda, I started the meeting by asking what I could do for her.

To my surprise, she began to talk about corporate social responsibility. She was passionate about helping underserved kids get better education, and she had been thinking a lot about how the company could make an impact in that area. The ideas were pouring out of her with great energy and excitement—and no sign of stopping.

I could see that my note-taker was alarmed at how the conversation had "derailed" the plan, but I wasn't worried. I just listened with genuine interest and offered to connect her with someone I knew who could help her get this initiative off the ground. After about 30 minutes, I said, "Listen, I have this list of questions for you, but we only have 15 minutes left. Do you want to do it another time?"

She said, "No, let's do it!" In the next 15 minutes, I got absolutely everything I needed from her.

If I knew exactly what I needed to get from the meeting, why did I approach it in this seemingly backward and inefficient way? The answer: *to build a relationship.* If I had treated the conversation like an interview (as my note-taker expected me to do), it would have been a transactional exchange of information. Instead, I took the time to build trust and goodwill by making my client feel valued, while demonstrating my own value at the same time. I made a real human connection.

There's incredible power in this kind of relationship. Your ability to access opportunities, get things done, be in the know, have influence, and make an impact all comes down to the strength of your network. Contrary to popular wisdom, it's not about shaking hands and banking favors with people in high places. It's about cultivating genuine rapport with diverse individuals who bring different kinds of value to the table. It's about expanding your *relationship radius.*

## Transactional and Exhausting

Social interaction in the modern workplace is—to put it bluntly—not much fun.

Remote and hybrid work are partly to blame. We spend more time staring at screens and talking into microphones than we do in face-to-face conversations, and the difference is very real. When you're not in person, there's no opportunity for casual chit-chat while you're waiting for a meeting to start, walking down the hall, getting coffee in the break room, or having lunch in the cafeteria. Plus, there's no real eye contact, and you miss out on an abundance of body language.

This leaves you feeling isolated and invisible. You don't really know who your colleagues are as people, and you feel like they don't really know you. Your sense of belonging and connection with your team is weak at best. You don't get enough feedback on how you're doing in your role, so you might feel uncertain about your job security and value to the company. In short, your social agency is fragile at best, nonexistent at worst.

However, we're all still having *lots* of interactions at work—more than ever, if you count emails and messages. Today's average white-collar worker will have one-on-one interactions with 12 to 15 people every day. The question is, how many of these interactions do they look forward to?

For most people, the answer is close to none. That's because a vast majority of these interactions are transactional; you want something from them, or they want something from you, or both. Information, opinions, ideas, approval, time, money, tools, effort—we're all just trying to get what we need to do our jobs. Even when someone just invites you to meet for coffee, you wonder what they really want from you.

This constant negotiation of wants and needs puts you in fight-or-flight mode.

> You're fighting to get what you want, or you're fleeing to avoid giving what they want.

I don't mean this literally, of course. But psychologically, whether you're asking for something or being asked, you're looking to protect yourself and your interests. It's a stressed state of mind.

This is incredibly draining. If you have 12 to 15 of those interactions in a day, you'll be mentally and emotionally exhausted. You'll even feel physically tired because those stress hormones take a very real toll on your body. Plus, in all those interactions, you never genuinely connect with the other person because you're both too focused on the takeaway. On top of that, there's the fact that people are switching jobs and companies more frequently than ever, so the people you're interacting with keep changing.

Given all this, it's no surprise that recent studies show that many young people are saying 'no' to meeting work colleagues after work. They have no energy left to socialize, especially with people whom they feel are just little more than strangers.

The bottom line is that in modern work, the number of interactions has gone up, but each one is more transactional. That leaves people feeling more socially disconnected than ever. The external conditions here are not going to change; we will continue to have hybrid work and a highly mobile workforce. So, how can we make those conditions work for us? How do we build social agency with each interaction instead of depleting it?

## Tend and Befriend

To answer that question, let me tell you about a consultant I work with, Samantha. She is routinely considered by her superiors to be one of the most resourceful people on the team. She gets things done fast, on a large scale. Everyone knows her and will gladly do something to help her. She's one of the few people about whom people speak positively behind her back. To everyone around her, it almost feels like she has some kind of magic wand for solving problems and making things happen.

Those are all signs that Samantha is world-class at managing her social agency. What does she do to cultivate this network of genuinely positive relationships that enables her to be both more effective *and* happier at work? She's a master of what I call *reverse networking*.

In modern work, you're a node in a network. As you know—in this world of complexity and fast-paced change—your ability to accomplish anything is highly dependent on other nodes. The better connected you are to the network, the easier it will be to get things done, and the bigger your impact will be.

> The better connected you are to the network,
> the easier it will be to get things done, and
> the bigger your impact will be.

In this, as in so many things in life, quality is more important than quantity. Running around shaking hands and collecting business cards will not create the kind of lasting, fruitful connections Samantha has. Instead, you need to build genuine, human relationships based on mutual trust and care.

The fastest and best way to do that is by participating in the agency of others. That means approaching every interaction with the question I asked my client at the beginning of this chapter: what can I do for you?

To be perfectly clear, you are *not* trying to bank favors. You're not offering to help other people with the expectation that they will "owe you one" and pay you back in some way. In fact, to do this properly, you must let go of your own agenda entirely. Forget about what you want and just show genuine interest in the other person and their priorities.

The goal here is to turn *off* the fight-or-flight response. As you just learned, that's the default mindset for both parties in most one-on-one interactions at work. To get the other person—and yourself—out of that stressed and defensive state of mind, you have to "tend and befriend."

To understand what I mean, think of an animal that has had a bad experience with humans. Its default mindset is to treat you as a threat, and if you try to get it to do anything, it will either lash out or shrink away. The only way to make any progress is to take care of it. Give it what it wants and needs—food, water, kindness, calm energy, positive attention—without making any demands of it. Do this consistently, and the animal will learn that you are safe and trustworthy. Once that relationship of trust is in place, it will be eager to do things for you— sit, walk, and cuddle—that were initially out of the question.

Today's workforce is hyper anxious. Every interaction is viewed as a potential threat, a source of fresh anxiety. For this reason, the animal analogy (sadly) works more or less the same way with people. When you genuinely listen to them, prioritize their needs, and treat them like human beings instead of resources, it immediately switches their state of mind from "threatened" to "safe." That switch happens automatically, without them having to think about it or choose. Instead of being suspicious and defensive, they begin to feel trusting and open. They become far more willing to share their time, knowledge, and more, not because they feel indebted to you but because they know, like, and trust you.

This has become the way I approach every meeting. I still prepare and create an agenda, but once I walk in, I let go of that agenda. If the other person wants to talk about something else, I go with that. I switch my brain from transactional mode (*What do I want?*) to tend-and-befriend mode (*How can I be of service?*). This immediately creates the potential for my agency and their agency to connect.

> This immediately creates the potential for my
> agency and their agency to connect.

Even when the other person approaches the interaction with hostility or skepticism, I've found that if you have the patience to persistently tend and befriend, they will eventually open up. For example, I had a meeting with a very senior, self-made businessman, and I opened (as usual) by asking what I could do for him. He became quite suspicious and said it was my job to tell him how I could add value to his organization. Instead of defending myself, I simply told him, "I won't presume to say anything about how I could add value because I don't know you or your business, so I'll let you speak."

There was a long, uncomfortable silence. I think we sat there without speaking for more than a minute (and in that situation, 60 seconds is a *long* time). But I was determined to let him speak first, and eventually, he did. In fact, he ended up talking almost continuously for about 90 minutes about his business and the challenges it was facing.

I won't pretend this will work every time. However, I do know that if you want to cultivate mutual trust, respect, and goodwill with another person, your best bet is to start by asking what you can do for them. Once you participate in their agency, they're much more likely to want to participate in yours.

## Beyond Your Inner Circle

You already have a core network of genuine relationships in your life: your family, your close friends, maybe your immediate team or department. This is your inner circle, and their support is important in your day-to-day life and work. However, in most cases, your inner circle doesn't do much to advance your social agency. They usually have a great deal in common with you; they share similar interests, skill sets, backgrounds, perspectives, and social networks. In that sense, your inner circle has a small radius.

Expanding your social agency means increasing that radius—going beyond the comfort zone of people who are easily reachable and similar to you. People within that comfort zone may provide excellent social support, but they probably won't open new doors for you. They probably won't inspire you with unfamiliar and unexpected ideas. They probably won't challenge you to do things in a different way. In other words, in many cases, you can't rely on your inner circle to multiply your social agency.

So, who *can* multiply it? People who are different from you—people who bring something to the table that you don't already have. Think broadly here; we're not just talking about power and influence but also resources, connections, skills, ideas, and perspectives. In terms of hierarchy or seniority, don't just look up. There's value to be found all around—up, down, and to the side.

To figure out who would make a valuable addition to your network of relationships, you have to go back to your personal agency. What matters to you? What are you trying to achieve? Keep an eye out for people who can help you move in that direction. You may find them in your office, at a conference, in your neighborhood—you never know where a valuable person might pop up.

The more important and more difficult question is, what do you do when you find them?

When you meet someone you want to connect with on a human level, remember that we live in a transactional world. Most people expect, by default, that you want something from them, and they have their guard up against that. To break through that barrier, you have to do something unexpected: offer them your genuine interest, attention, and help, no strings attached. Without this element of surprise, you'll have a hard time taking the interaction beyond the transactional level.

Note that this isn't the same as offering *value*. We're all constantly bombarded with offers of "free" value—discounts, exclusive access, information, advice, etc. We know fully well that they're not free. On the other side is someone hoping to get something back from us, if only our email address. When you offer anything of value that the other person hasn't asked for, it feels like a trap, not a gift.

Even when you provide value that they *have* asked for, the relationship may still be transactional. I've seen this over and over as a consultant. My team and I can provide millions of dollars' worth of value, even save a client's company or job, and then they simply pay the bill and move on. If I haven't taken the time to forge that human connection, there's no real relationship—nothing to endure beyond the agreed-upon exchange of value.

So how do you break out of this transactional value exchange? The answer lies in reverse networking, where you build relationships without an exchange of value—simply by shifting your focus from adding or exchanging value to making the person feel valued.

## Reverse Networking Will Transform Your Relationships

Reverse networking isn't about providing value to the other person; it's about making them *feel valued* by you. And expanding your relationship radius is about doing that strategically with people who can multiply your impact. If you can convert even one third of your interactions into reverse networking, your work life will transform in four key ways.

Reverse networking isn't about providing value
to the other person; it's about making
them *feel valued* by you.

## (1) More positive interactions every day

Right now, workplace interactions are likely a major source of stress and negative emotions. You probably dream of a day free of meetings, emails, and messages. I even know people whose favorite days to work are national holidays, when everyone else is taking the day off.

However, when you have the genuine human connections that come from reverse networking, you'll start to lean into social interactions instead of away from them. Conversations will boost your energy instead of draining it. You'll anticipate good things from other people.

This makes a gigantic difference in your mental and emotional state at work. You will, quite simply, *feel better*—more energized, motivated, optimistic, and empowered. That by itself goes a long way toward combating the overwhelm, frustration, and anxiety we talked about at the beginning of this book.

## (2) More support, collaboration, and opportunities

In addition to feeling better, you'll have an easier time getting things done and making the impact you want to make because you'll have more allies. When you actively participate in other people's agency, they will want to actively participate in yours. Instead of friction everywhere, you'll begin to see help, support, and collaboration—green lights instead of red.

You'll also *notice* more opportunities simply because you're giving other people more space to talk about their needs and even aspirations. When you focus on getting what you want from others, it's like plowing through the world with blinders and headphones on— everything but your intended destination is blocked out. Reverse networking forces you to take those blinders and headphones off, slow down, and let the rest of the world in. You'll be shocked at how many fascinating problems and projects land at your feet just because you give them space.

## (3) More success in the marketplace of skills

In the modern workplace, you're constantly having to prove your value. The clear hierarchy and career track is disappearing, being replaced by a system where your access to projects and opportunities is directly tied to the value you can bring. It's not necessarily a bad thing; for top talent, it provides a much faster upward trajectory. However, if you don't know how to show your value, you won't get picked for the team.

Reverse networking gives you the opportunity to show your talent by creating value for others in the ways they care about the most. Think of Samantha; based on what I shared with you, do you think she's in high demand in our marketplace of skills? You bet she is! She's proven over and over, to many different people, that she can understand and fulfill their needs. Everyone knows what she's capable of, and on top of that, they enjoy working with her. That gives her a massive leg up in a highly competitive organization.

## (4) Better access to knowledge

With the rise of remote work, it has become increasingly hard to disseminate institutional knowledge. Our knowledge management systems can't keep up with the rate of change and learning; at my own firm, our system is designed to be updated a few times in a year. That means there's 2–3 months of new knowledge that can only be accessed by talking to someone who already knows it.

Without casual in-person interactions, it's tough to figure out where to get the information you need, or to even become aware that you're missing information in the first place. That's especially true when you're new to an organization or role. When I talk to the cohort of young talent at my firm, they say one of the biggest sources of overwhelm is the constant search for the right internal knowledge.

If the most up-to-date knowledge is in the heads of people around you, it becomes incredibly important to build your connections with those people. It doesn't have to be a lot—10–15 strategic, quality connections are usually enough to become very well embedded in the workplace social/information network.

Again, reverse networking is the critical tool here because transactional interactions are not enough. You can't just walk up to these people and ask them to give you information because you don't even know what you need, and neither do they. Instead of repeatedly going on fact-finding missions, build and maintain genuine relationships with these key people by serving their needs first. Then, when they become aware of what you're working on and trying to achieve, they will voluntarily connect you with the people and resources you need.

## Reverse Networking Don'ts

As you begin to practice this rule, keep in mind three things you should NOT do.

### (1) Don't be one-sided.

Social agency only works as a two-way flow: you participate in other people's agency and they participate in yours. If the balance gets off, the symbiotic relationship falls apart. So, don't get greedy. Don't start the relationship by giving and then assume it's all receiving from there on out. Trust requires maintenance. Keep listening, keep asking how you can help, and when they extend you an invitation to participate in their agency, accept it gladly, not grudgingly. It sounds very kindergarten, but to put it simply, treat others the way you want to be treated.

### (2) Don't be fake.

Your interest in others and your desire to serve their needs *must* be genuine. If you think you can fake your way through this to get to the payoff, think again. People can smell a fake a mile away, even unconsciously. Even if you say the "right" things, the lack of sincerity will come through in your body language and tone of voice. Instead of making the other person feel safe, you'll make them even more suspicious. There's no way their brain will make the switch from fight-or-flight to tend-and-befriend.

So, before you enter a reverse networking interaction, take a moment to put your mind in the right place. Remind yourself that your goal in this conversation is NOT to get what you want or push your agenda. It's to build trust with the other person—and the best way to do that is to listen to them and participate in their agency in whatever way you can.

## (3) Don't be hierarchical.

In networking of any kind, there's always a temptation to focus on the people above you—the ones who have more status, more power, and more resources to help you climb the ladder. It's certainly beneficial to build trusting relationships with those people. However, don't stop there. The strongest nodes in a network are the ones that have connections in *every* direction—up, down, and sideways.

That's because, when it comes to achieving the things you care about, you'll need help from all sides. People above you can provide things like exposure, funding, and advice. But for active collaboration and honest feedback, you're better off looking toward your peers. For help with time-consuming tasks like research, testing, and implementation, your junior colleagues might be the best resource. No matter where a person stands relative to you in the corporate landscape, they have value to offer.

This is especially important for mid-level team leaders to understand. Yes, the people above you can help you get things done... but so can your team members. That's what they're there for! And they will put in a lot more effort for you if they *know* you actually care about them, because you've bothered to get to know them and help them do the things *they* care about. In fact, reverse networking downward can help you attract and retain higher quality team members because you'll become the type of boss people actually want to work for and work with.

## Conclusion

For me, reverse networking has become a way of life. I still have my goals and agendas, but I've learned to recognize that so does everybody else. That's not an obstacle—it's an opportunity. Most people never even get to fully express what they want to achieve, much less receive an unsolicited offer of support. By putting my agenda aside for a moment to give others that time or chance to think about theirs, I am able to build trust and respect that pay massive benefits in the long run. Ironically, since I stopped pushing my agenda, it has become much easier to accomplish it.

> Ironically, since I stopped pushing my agenda,
> it has become much easier to accomplish it.

The bonus is the impact on my personal agency. My stress expectation from interpersonal interactions has become nearly non-existent. That may seem crazy, but it just speaks to how much of that stress was coming from the friction of interpersonal interactions. Without realizing it, I was in fight-or-flight mode in nearly all my conversations, and so were the people on the other side. When I learned to switch to tend-and-befriend, all that stress disappeared.

This is the first and most essential step in growing your social agency. It's impossible to overstate the value of the relationships you'll build this way. They will make you happier. They will multiply your impact. They will open doors to futures you would never have imagined for yourself. The ROI is practically infinite.

And yet, the journey to maximize your social agency isn't over yet. The next two chapters will show you how you can become an even greater master of this powerful skill.

# VISUAL SUMMARY : EXPAND YOUR RELATIONSHIP RADIUS

"Thank you for reaching out and offering to help"

"Your spreadsheet was a huge help in the meeting"

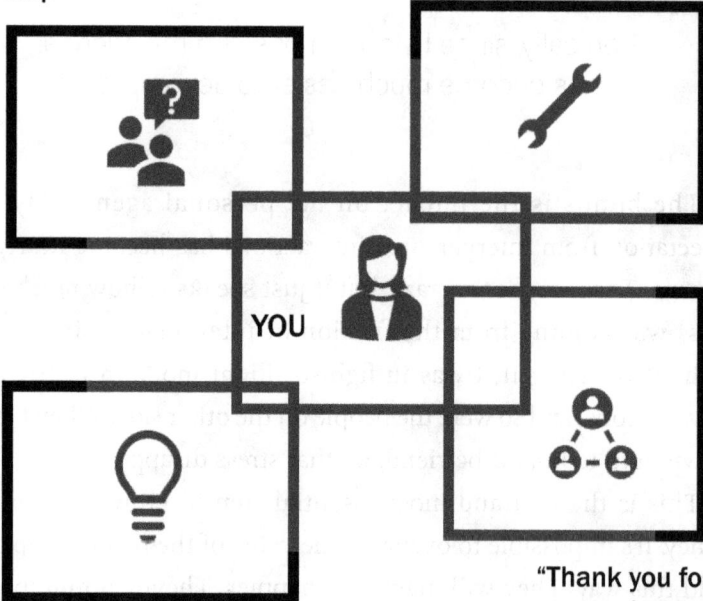

YOU

"Thank you for connecting me with Joanna"

"You posted a link to the video ... it gave me the insights I needed"

# 09 | Rule #6: Seek Out Difference

L ast year, one of my clients came to me with a problem. The complexity of his business was escalating, but his teams were struggling to collaborate effectively. Working together across teams had become a costly source of friction in the organization, slowing down their ability to make decisions and get things done. He wanted my help in finding a way to make collaboration smoother and easier for everyone.

So, we started with a broad survey across the company, asking over a hundred questions about how people were really operating day to day. Among those were two questions:

1.  What does it feel like to collaborate within your immediate team?
2.  What does it feel like to collaborate with another function?

The first question had the best average score of all the items in the survey. The second question had the worst.

The execs were stunned for a moment... but then someone said, "Wait, remember what happened last week?" It turns out, the executive team had come close to violence in a discussion over a proposed project. Some of them insisted on the importance of minimizing costs to ensure financial success; others insisted on minimizing the environmental impact, which would add costs. The conflict had been heated, and ultimately, inconclusive.

These kinds of battles get waged across functions every day, in big and small ways. Sometimes they simmer under the surface for long periods; on occasion they boil over dramatically. If you ask why, both sides will say things like: *Those people are impossible. They just don't understand. They don't listen. They're selfish. They're unreasonable. They don't see the bigger picture.*

What's really going on is that different people *perceive the world* differently. They focus on different pieces of information, prioritize different goals, make different assumptions, and reason in different ways. It all depends on their natural tendencies and preferences, as well as their previous training and experience.

> What's really going on is that different people
> *perceive the world* differently.

Within a given function, these differences tend to be small. People tend to think similarly because they have similar backgrounds and skill sets. Plus, they spend more time together and so they are more likely to give each other the benefit of doubt when there seems to be a disagreement.

Across functions is where you'll find major gaps—sometimes gaping chasms—between perspectives on a problem. These differences are often so inexplicable that each party concludes the other person must be either an idiot or a jerk. There seems to be no other plausible reason for the conflict.

Rule #6 is designed to address this problem. It tells you that instead of avoiding or resisting diverse thinking, you should *seek it out*. In a world of escalating complexity, every significant problem requires multiple perspectives and skill sets. The only way to get comfortable operating in that world is to *practice*, and to do so with conscious awareness that not only can other people's perspectives, while different from your own, be valid but also valuable.

## Four Vectors of Complexity

Until very recently, most organizational design reflected the Henry Ford model of productivity. In Ford's assembly lines, complex jobs were broken down into simple, easily repeatable tasks that required only a narrow skill set. To varying degrees, most organizations do something similar: they create functions for specific types of tasks, populated by people with the same skill set. There have been some tweaks to that, like the matrix organization that creates explicit ties across functions. But even then, at the end of the day, most people "grow up" in the corporate world inside one area of specialization.

That's fine if the problems at hand are relatively one-dimensional. But as we've established, that's not the world we live in anymore. In virtually every kind of business, all around the globe, complexity is on the rise—and it's multidimensional.

In any business problem, there are four possible vectors of complexity.

The first is **desirability**: how do I make it desirable to the user? How do I make this product desirable to the consumer? How do I make this company policy desirable to employees? How do I make this report desirable to the executive team? In the traditional organizational model, desirability is viewed as the purview of the marketing department.

The second vector is **feasibility**: how do I make it work well? Is it technically possible? How do I make it efficient and robust? How do I minimize the possibility of errors and breakdowns? This is the primary focus of departments like production, IT, engineering, or operations.

The third vector is **viability**: how do I make it profitable? Is there a market for it? Will people pay for it? Is it worth the cost? Does it produce a return on investment? This is the domain of the finance department.

The fourth vector is **sustainability**: how do I minimize harm? Does it have adverse impacts on people and the environment? Over time, will it have a net positive impact on all stakeholders? This is much more important today than it was in the past. Traditionally, it was the concern of the PR department, if it was a concern at all.

Most people only learn to operate along *one* of these vectors. Even people who have had long and varied careers typically default to just one way of thinking. It's remarkably consistent across the thousands of executives I've worked with over the years; everyone has their go-to way of looking at the world. In most cases, that perspective aligns with their education and early career. People who got their start in technical areas like engineering tend to be focused on feasibility, people who started in marketing lean toward desirability, and so on.

## The Stress of Dependency

When a problem involves multiple vectors of complexity, different ways of thinking must come together.

For example, I recently met with a group of seven executives who are planning a major business transformation. Three of them were focused on feasibility; they wanted to talk about all the ways the project could go wrong and how to minimize the risks. Another three were focused on desirability; they wanted to talk about crafting the right narrative to get buy-in from shareholders, employees, and other stakeholders. The lead executive, a finance person, was primarily concerned with viability; he wanted to get clear on the business case for the transformation, especially because the organization had lost money on transformations before.

In short, there were three completely separate conversations happening in that room. Each group felt that the others were not listening and not paying attention to what really mattered. Unsurprisingly, this dynamic was incredibly frustrating for everyone.

That's a perfect illustration of why personal agency alone isn't enough to thrive at work. Senior executives typically have pretty strong personal agency on their own; when they talk to me about what's holding them back at work, it's almost always about *dependency*. They feel their success and fulfillment is dependent on other people—people they don't see eye to eye with. As a result, their sense of control and efficacy crumbles in collaborative settings.

Over and over, I hear my clients say that collaboration is the problem. Let's be more precise. Collaboration is fun, easy, and exciting when you're working with people you like and understand—people who think the way you do, usually people from your own department or area of expertise. However, in modern work, almost all productive collaboration requires you to work with people from other disciplines—people whose default vector of complexity is different from yours. You don't understand the way they think and vice versa, so you're constantly at odds with each other.

This reaction is deeply emotional. For example, if you see things from a desirability perspective, you probably think of yourself as creative, empathetic, and open. People who share your worldview will agree. However, someone who comes from a feasibility perspective will perceive you as out of touch with practical realities, risky, and wasteful. That person thinks of themselves as smart, realistic, efficient, and resourceful. You see them as unimaginative, negative, detail-obsessed, and out of touch with people.

The sustainability thinkers probably get the worst reputation of all. Everyone else views them as unrealistic, idealistic, and impractical. They're thinking... *We don't have time for this—we'll worry about sustainability when everything else has been solved.* At the same time, the sustainability people are thinking... *We have to talk about this now, before it's too late to make this thing sustainable.*

These emotional reactions are deep, strong, and immediate. That's why so many people find it so difficult to collaborate across disciplines. You would think we would learn to see things from other perspectives... but when does anyone teach us that? When do we practice it?

## Build Your Collaboration Muscle

Whenever you're trying to get anything significant done at work, you're going to bump into a different perspective from yours. This is the reality of modern work, and it's not going away anytime soon. The only thing we can do is try to get better at operating under these conditions.

The intellectual way of dealing with this problem doesn't work very well. I've tried all manner of coaching, counseling, and mediation to help both my clients and my own firm get better at cross-functional collaboration. It works for a few minutes, but then everyone leaves the meeting and goes back into their own world, surrounded by their own kind of thinkers. There, they immediately reinforce their own perspectives, and all the good work that was done together goes out the window.

What we need is a social/emotional approach, one that reaches beyond cognitive understanding and actually builds the "muscle" of collaboration. The only way to do that is to intentionally surround yourself with different types of thinkers as often as possible. Ideally, this means being part of at least one team that includes at least three out of the four perspectives: desirability, feasibility, viability, and sustainability. Cross-functional collaboration is a skill, and it's an absolutely crucial one for achieving a robust sense of social agency. Just like a muscle, it can only become strong and reliable through consistent, deliberate practice.

It will be challenging at first because you will not naturally get along with your collaborators. In my experience, it takes 3 to 4 months of practice to get comfortable. The first month is torture; you'll feel like the debates never end and nothing ever gets anywhere. In the second month, some sort of understanding and tolerance will develop, and you'll start to be able to predict what the others are going to say. In the third month, you get used to the rhythm of the debate and find ways to compromise. By the fourth month, you see the value in their ways of thinking, and the collaboration starts to flow much faster.

I've led executive teams through this process multiple times. They are the prototypical cross-functional team, where the leaders of each function come together to make critical strategic decisions for the company. They may meet regularly, but without any awareness or understanding of the differences in their ways of thinking, those meetings often turn into unproductive battles.

However, with some guidance, those meetings can become the perfect opportunity for deliberate practice of cross-functional collaboration skills. When that mental shift happens, the transformation is remarkable. Decisions that used to take 8 months now take only 2 weeks. Meetings that used to be pitched battles become productive— even *fun*—work sessions. People who used to treat each other as foes learn to see each other as resources.

The best type of teams for this are *product* teams, because to successfully create, launch, and manage a product, the team must consider all four vectors of complexity. In fact, the best way for leaders to institutionalize this rule is to structure the organization as a group of product teams. These teams typically include designers and marketers who take a desirability perspective, engineers and operators who take a feasibility perspective, and accountants and business managers who take a viability perspective.

Ideally, they should also include someone with a sustainability perspective. This is still a relatively new role, and it often falls to someone who is mandated to think about the long-term consequences of business activities. However, even if there's no team member whose explicit job is to focus on sustainability, it's important to have someone who tends to think in terms of broad impacts.[1]

Even if you're in a global function like HR or finance, you can still create this kind of multi-perspective team; you don't actually need a product to have a product team. You just need something you can *treat* like a product—a project, a process, a policy, a tool. The moment you treat something like a product, you can design a multidisciplinary team around it.

---

[1] It's worth noting that there are often cultural differences around the treatment of sustainability. In my experience, when organizations from western cultures talk about the "long term," that typically means 5-10 years out. However, eastern cultures tend to take a much longer view—30, 40, or even 50 years out. This is also often true of family businesses where ownership has passed from generation to generation.

For example, let's say you're in finance, and your mission is to improve the quarterly report. What if you treat it like a product? Bring in someone with a customer service or marketing background to find out who is reading the report and what they're trying to get from it. Someone with a technical background can help with accuracy, clarity, flow, and formatting. Someone with a financial perspective can help manage the report's financial impact—its ability to help the company raise or manage money. Someone with a sustainability perspective can think about the downstream impacts of the report, like who it affects and what unintended consequences it might have.

What if you have no authority to create a team like that? In an ideal world, you would be able to create or participate in a product team, or at least a mock-product team. If that's not a possibility for you, look for volunteer opportunities where different perspectives are likely to come together: a policy committee, a party planning committee, or an office move or renovation committee.

You can also look for ways to surround yourself with different types of thinkers *outside* of work. This relates closely to Rule #10: run a side hustle. If you're working on a meaningful project outside of work, that's an excellent opportunity to collaborate with people who have different backgrounds and perspectives. (More on that later.)

But even aside from a side hustle, you can apply this rule in your social life. Figure out what your natural inclination is among the four vectors, pick the extreme opposite, and spend time with those people. Really listen to the way they approach the problems they face in their lives. Ask questions to get a deeper understanding of the information they pay attention to, the things they prioritize, and the way they reason.

For example, my default perspective is a combination of desirability and feasibility, with a somewhat stronger emphasis on desirability. I rarely focus on viability. So, I try to spend as much time as possible with early-stage founders, who tend to be *highly* focused on viability because they're worried about how to make ends meet every month. Short-term cash flow problems are what keep them up at night. Just by hanging out with those people, I've learned so much about how they think and process information, which has made a huge difference in how I'm able to advise my clients.

## Understand Your Own Perspective

Understanding and acknowledging your own perspective is one of the most liberating and joyful things you can do for yourself. You get to stop thinking you're always right and everyone else is always wrong—a belief that usually leaves you feeling frustrated, hopeless, or infuriated. You can stop wasting time shutting other people down, escalating conflict, or withdrawing from important conversations. All that negative energy around collaboration can just disappear, simply by acknowledging the nature of your own thinking and becoming *curious* about the nature of other people's thinking.

Usually, your default perspective is obvious, but a few times, I've met people who had a hard time self-identifying. This is usually because there's some mismatch between how they naturally think and what they were trained to do. For example, one of those people was educated as an engineer but never really loved that role; he was trained to think from a feasibility perspective, but naturally, he actually gravitated toward viability. He later turned out to be a great private equity professional.

It's exceedingly rare for someone to be equally comfortable with all four perspectives. Among the thousands of people I've worked with, there are less than 20 who genuinely played across three different vectors, and none who used all four. More likely, you have one perspective that feels very natural to you and some lesser degree of comfort with one or two others. Don't worry about mastering or adopting all four vectors for yourself. You just need to be able to acknowledge and fully consider the value of the other perspectives when people bring them to the table.

## Some Practical Collaboration Advice

As you seek out different styles of thinking and practice understanding those unfamiliar perspectives, there are a few things to keep in mind.

### (1) You may run into some hopeless cases.

Even if you invest heavily in cultivating your collaboration skills, you may still find that there are some people you struggle to work with.

I've worked extremely hard to surround myself with different perspectives. I've studied and worked in both engineering (feasibility) and psychology (desirability). The consultants on my team are virtually all from different generations than I am. The leadership team I'm part of is mostly women. As I mentioned earlier, I make specific efforts to spend time with people who think in ways I find uncomfortable, like startup founders. I've really gone all-in on this rule... and yet, there are still a handful of people I just can't figure out, even after years of trying.

Although they may seem quite different from each other on the surface, these difficult people have something in common: an unwillingness to be *vulnerable.*

Vulnerability is required for authentic collaboration. You must be willing to openly recognize that you don't know everything, and you could be wrong. You have to be able to say things like, "I didn't think of it like that. Now that I do, it makes sense. I see what you mean." As a rule, people don't love to be vulnerable like that, but in most cases, they will relax and open up in the presence of others who do the same.

By being vulnerable yourself, you make it easier for other people to be vulnerable with you.

However, some people will just not let their guard down. On the surface, this comes off as arrogance, condescension, or dismissiveness; they simply refuse to entertain the possibility that they might not be seeing the full picture. Deep down, this kind of behavior is usually driven by insecurity. Their self-image doesn't match the image they want to project to the world, so they put on a facade of unshakeable confidence.

That makes it very hard to collaborate fully and authentically. No matter how hard you try to see things from their perspective, they will not reciprocate, and it will end up feeling like you're constantly butting heads. Unfortunately, there's very little you can do about this; you can only control your behavior, not theirs, and this kind of deep-seated psychological barrier is not your problem to solve. Your best bet is to focus on the people who *are* willing to collaborate and hope that those interactions set a persuasive example.

## (2) This skill applies to all types of diversity.

We've been talking a lot about diversity of thinking styles, but of course, there are many other kinds of diversity—gender, age, ethnicity, culture, etc. Once you develop the skill of collaborating with people who think differently, you'll find many opportunities to apply it to those kinds of differences as well. You'll be much better able to look beyond first impressions and stereotypes to see the full value other people bring to the table.

That said, it's worth noting that just because there is *visible* diversity in a group doesn't mean there is diversity of *thinking*. You could easily have a team of people who seem different on the surface, but all think in terms of the same vector of complexity; it happens all the time within functions. That's not a bad thing at all. However, to get the fullest perspective on a problem and come up with the most creative and robust solution, diversity of thinking is crucial.

For example, I've learned to love working with my Gen Z team members precisely because they think differently than I do. Their generation is often characterized as impatient, entitled, fragile, anxious, and selfish. However, the more I genuinely engage with them and understand how they think, the more value I get from their perspective.

For example, this generation has been taught by their environment not to wait. Everything has always been at their fingertips the moment they want it—online shopping, streaming, delivery, etc. This "impatience" led to real innovation when my team started to wonder why corporate culture statements all seemed to say the same things. Using traditional methods, it would have taken a year to do meaningful research on the subject, and we didn't want to invest in such a large effort. But in a matter of days, my young Gen Z analysts used a web crawler to gather culture statements from the top 100 companies in the world. Within a couple weeks, we had analyzed the language and created a "periodic table" of culture. If I hadn't valued their way of thinking, this project would never have happened at all.

### (3) Vectors of complexity can be points of social connection.

When you focus on diversity of thinking, you might find that people who seem strikingly different from you on the surface actually think the same way you do, which helps you to connect with them on a deeper level. For example, early in my career, I went from North India—a place largely characterized by dense urbanity and toxic masculinity—to the Midwest United States, a place that's mostly agricultural and known for its friendly culture. It was like being on a different planet. And yet, there was a feasibility bent to the Midwestern attitude—a concern with quality of process, repeatability, and robustness—that resonated with my engineering-trained mind. Once I understood that, I didn't feel so out of place.

## Conclusion

I'll be perfectly honest with you: this is probably the most emotionally challenging of the ten rules to master. Most of us regularly encounter different styles of thinking at work; that's exactly why at times, we experience so much interpersonal conflict. However, it takes dedication to transform those encounters into opportunities to practice collaboration. It's often painful at first, especially if you're trying to heal long-standing rifts between teams and departments with a history of conflict.

However, the ability to truly collaborate with people who think differently from you will pay immeasurable dividends over the long run. You'll experience less conflict, which means less stress and negativity in your daily work life. When you face complex problems, you'll come up with better solutions and implement them faster, which makes the whole company more agile and competitive—and makes you more valuable to the company. Approach this rule with curiosity and patience, and you'll be well rewarded for your efforts.

# VISUAL SUMMARY : SEEK OUT DIFFERENCE

## TRADITIONAL (FUNCTIONAL) TEAMS

**ONE** PERSPECTIVE

- ❌ DESIRABILITY
- ❌ FEASIBILITY
- ❌ VIABILITY
- ✅ SUSTAINABILITY

Risk Professional

Risk Professional

Risk Professional

Risk Professional

YOU

Financial Professional

Operational Professional

Design Professional

**FOUR** PERSPECTIVES

- ✅ DESIRABILITY
- ✅ FEASIBILITY
- ✅ VIABILITY
- ✅ SUSTAINABILITY

## MODERN TEAMS

# 10 | Rule #7: Build a Personal Board of Advisors

igh agency individuals constantly expand their relationship radius and actively collaborate with people who think differently from them. As I have coached young talent and senior executives on building their social agency, one thing has become clear to me.

In today's world of constantly changing capabilities, viewpoints, and perspectives, you need to do something that only large companies do systematically. Create a board of directors or advisors who will bring genuine insights into critical aspects of the business in a mindful, structured way to the table.

This is the so-called holy grail of social agency. It is difficult to do, even more challenging to grow and evolve, but it is something the highest-agency people all have in common: a personal board of advisors.

We've already established that the pace of change in today's world is unprecedented; you're probably sick of hearing about it by now. There seems to be an endless flood of new developments in every field, every day. On top of that, the amount of information coming at you from all directions has exploded. Every time you look for an answer to a question, you have to sort through a sea of voices, many of which seem to be at odds with each other.

Obviously, the upside of all this is that whatever you want to learn, you can. Accessing information is easier than ever. The hard part is figuring out what information is important and what isn't. That takes time (which we're all short on), as well as a keen sense of judgment honed through experience (which we only have in our own areas of expertise).

The bottom line is, it has become impossible to keep up with important developments all on your own. There's simply too much going on and too much being said about it. You could spend all day, every day reading and still not manage it—and of course, you can't do that. You have a job to do and a life to live.

The solution is a personal board of advisors: a small group of experts who let you periodically pick their brains. This only takes a small investment of time, but the return on that investment is enormous.

## Cut Through the Noise

This whole journey toward higher agency started with the feeling of being overwhelmed, and a big slice of that feeling is related to learning. The sense of urgency around keeping up is overwhelming, and the plethora of learning options only amplifies that feeling. What should you focus on? Who should you listen to? What really matters, and what will turn out to be irrelevant or just plain wrong? How are you supposed to make that call?

This is especially difficult when you're talking about new ideas that are still under development, like blockchain and AI. Not only are things constantly evolving—new tech, new players, new applications—but there's also a huge variety of opinions about it all. People are making predictions and value judgments left, right, and center. Some of those views are less informed and more biased than others... but how can you tell which to believe and which to discard?

Just take the world of nutrition, for example. This is not even a new field—people have been formally studying it for over a century—but advances in medical science have led to an explosion of theories, studies, and diets. Some say we should eat only plant-based foods; others say animal protein is the foundation of a healthy diet. Some believe that many small meals scattered throughout the day is best; others insist on the benefits of fasting for 16 hours every day. Some believe we should only eat raw foods; others say cooking is essential for breaking down toxins. These are just a few examples of the many contradictory nutrition philosophies, and each camp holds their views very strongly and uses data to support them.

In such a confusing landscape, the notions of "expert" and "truth" become very blurry. Mistakes and misdirection often come from highly educated and qualified people. Most of us don't have the time to dig into all those opinions and understand the raw data, so it's easy to get convinced by misinformation.

This is why it's so helpful to surround yourself with a handful of people you trust who have expertise in different areas. They can cut through the noise and steer you toward what's important—and away from what's not.

For example, a colleague and friend of mine, Irene, has a background in operations, and her work focused primarily on helping companies make their employees and processes more efficient. But several years ago, she became interested in cybersecurity because she was doing a lot of work with banks, which were concerned about being hacked. To learn more about this area, she included someone with cybersecurity expertise on her personal board of advisors.

Fast forward to now, and Irene is in the eye of the storm in the cybersecurity world. What was once a purely technological issue has now become a cultural issue as well, because companies have recognized that the biggest cybersecurity risks come from human behavior. Even the most sophisticated security systems can fall to malware when an employee picks up a USB drive marked "Home Videos" in the company parking lot and puts it in their corporate computer. Nikesh Arora, the CEO of Palo Alto Networks, uses this story as an example of human quirks being the ultimate threat to the world of cyber. Suddenly, organizations are seeking the help of behavioral experts who can help them address their *cultural* cybersecurity risks—and Irene is perfectly positioned to serve that need.

This isn't something she could have planned, and neither can you. You never know exactly how the people on your board of advisors—and the domains they expose you to—might put you in the right place at the right time, at the center of a boom of interest. But if you build a board that broadens your horizons in ways that genuinely interest you, you maximize your chances of sparking those big bursts of knowhow and insight.

This is the signature difference in the way high agency individuals operate. They don't try to go at it alone. Instead, they regularly seek out people who can help them make sense of the flood of information, providing a powerful shortcut to understanding the changing world around them.

## How to Build Your Board

Before you start building your personal board of advisors, let's make an important distinction. Advisors and mentors are not quite the same thing. The primary playbook of a mentor starts with the chapter "when

I was your age…" When you ask for mentorship from a person, you're giving them permission to take that perspective. There can be value in that, but it's not what we're looking for here.

An advisor is someone with expertise in an area where you have little knowledge and experience. Their purpose isn't to help guide your career, your professional development, or your personal growth. It's to share their perspective so you can quickly understand an unfamiliar but important worldview. This is different and separate from the role of a mentor.

It's to share their perspective so you can quickly understand an unfamiliar but important worldview.

To see the difference, think of the people surrounding a head of state. There are political advisors, economic advisors, public relations advisors, military advisors, domestic affairs advisors, international affairs advisors—you get the picture. Those people don't "mentor" the head of state. They synthesize huge amounts of complex information from their respective fields and pass it on to the head of state, so they can make informed decisions about how to lead the country.

So, how do you assemble this game-changing group of people for yourself?

First of all, it's never too early or too late to start. You can build a personal board of advisors at any time, even in college or your first job, and even if you're already decades into your career. The composition of the group will evolve with your professional life, reflecting your changing interests and levels of responsibility at work. The most important thing is to start where you are and not put it off.

Ideally, your board of advisors should include at least three people and probably not more than six. You want a variety of perspectives and expertise, so just a couple of people isn't quite enough. At the same time, you don't want to overwhelm yourself with excess information or conflicting views; that's exactly what we're trying to avoid. From my personal experience and my observations of many leaders who engage in this practice, a handful of advisors is about the right amount.

To identify the right people for your board, I recommend looking at four different factors.

- **The first is domain.** Obviously, your board of advisors should cover areas of expertise that are interesting and relevant to you but are beyond your current expertise. My personal yardstick for this is that I find myself obsessing over their domain—the more I learn, the more I want to know. I want the same to be true for them as well, so they get as much value out of our time together as I do.
- **The second factor is level.** Look for people who are one or two levels ahead of you in terms of their seniority, expertise, and impact. This is primarily for practical reasons; it's hard to get people who are very far ahead of you to commit to spending time with you. If you're well into your career, like me, you can probably also learn quite a lot from people who are one or two levels behind you but in a different domain.
- **The third factor is reach.** Look for people who have access to a wide variety of knowledge and people in their fields— people who enjoy reading widely and making connections

with their peers. They're going to be the ones who stay up to date on recent developments, have well-informed views on them, and can point you toward the best people and resources when you want to learn more.

- **The fourth and final factor is chemistry.** These are people you're going to spend time with on a regular basis, so you better like them, and they better like you! That mutual interest and rapport are essential to keep the relationship healthy and fun, so it doesn't feel like a burden to either party.

Where do you find these people? There's no limit. My personal board of advisors includes former classmates, colleagues, clients, and social contacts. If you practice the three rules of social agency—especially if you extend them to your life outside of work—you'll quickly build a network full of valuable people that could potentially be good advisors.

So, how do you actually invite someone to become part of your personal board? This is rarely, if ever, the very first step in the relationship. Typically, you will interact with the person in some other capacity first—perhaps as a colleague, friend, or client. That allows you to get to know them enough to see whether they meet the criteria we've just discussed. It also gives you time to build up some rapport with them and get a sense of whether they might be interested in spending more time with you.

By that point, the invitation is simple. Just say that you have a select group of people you reach out to on a regular basis for the purpose of exchanging ideas and staying up to date on various areas of interest, and you would love to include them in that group. Explain what the relationship could look like—how often you would meet and so on—and ask if they might be interested. If you're a young person inviting a more senior person, it often makes sense to position the relationship explicitly as a mentorship. Senior people tend to view mentoring as part of their responsibilities as a leader, and they may be open to mentoring a promising young person even if you don't feel you have much to offer them in return.

In any case, there's no need to overcomplicate this conversation. Simply reach out with a spirit of humility and generosity, and make *the ask*.

## My Board of Advisors

To show you how this can play out, I'd like to introduce you to *my* personal board of advisors and explain how I engage with them.

Ayush (not his real name) is the global CEO of a nutrition company, with professional experience in something like ten different countries. He is a role model for me in terms of what a CEO should look like: human-centric, deeply spiritual, and adept at balancing the interests of shareholders, employees, customers, the community, and the environment.

Allison (not her real name) is a top headhunter in the consumer industry, particularly in beauty and fashion. She's my guru on what's cool, trendy, and buzz worthy. She's also exceptionally savvy about C-suite and boardroom politics.

John (not his real name) is the CEO of a major international NGO focused on sustainability. He's one of the top ten thought leaders in the world on protecting the environment.

Govind (yup, this name is real) is a classmate from engineering school who is now the Head of Mathematics at an elite university. He's one of the leading thinkers on AI, particularly when it comes to ethics and policy.

Ronnie (not his real name) is a young CEO making bold moves in telecommunications and technology. He's my go-to person for understanding how young people can change the world.

Lena (not her real name) is the CEO of a startup that's aiming to disrupt the world of personal finance. She is my guide to anything related to Silicon Valley and technology.

Those are my six advisors, and I typically meet with each one individually about once every few months—maybe two to six times a year. We're all busy people, so I make the most of those meetings by structuring them around five types of questions: who, what, how, where, and so what?

Who:

- Who are the people you follow and why?
- Whose opinions do you respect?
- Who do you feel is getting it wrong and why?

What:

- What has become clearer to you since we last met? (This question helps them distill the insight that has crystallized for them so they're not spending a lot of time giving me opinions that aren't fully formed.)
- What are you paying attention to? What are you ignoring?
- What has surprised you since we last met?

How:

- How do you spend your time?
- How are you investing?
- How do you spend/refresh your energy?
- How are you navigating change?

Where:

- Where do you expect the next big thing? What industry, country, company, etc. should I be watching?
- Where do you see pockets of growth?
- Where are the risks?
- Where do you see real opportunities?

So what:

- If you were in my shoes, what moves would you make?
- What are the key things I should take away from this conversation?

The learning that comes from these conversations is truly mind-boggling. In my last conversation with Allison, we talked for 6 hours, and I swear I could *feel* my brain change. For me, it's truly a joy and a privilege to spend time with these people.

It may seem like the delivery of wisdom in these discussions is one-way, but my advisors actually do get something in return. Through my questions and our dialogue, they get to clarify their own thinking. I know this because that's the value I get when I act as an advisor to someone else. My advisors enjoy our conversations and get as much value out of them as I do, which is the key to maintaining a lasting relationship.

## Conclusion

Let me be clear: the idea of a personal board of advisors is not new or original. It's well-tested; there's even a Harvard Business Review paper on it (Stelter, 2022). It's just that very few people outside of the C-suite practice it.

The biggest barrier for most people is simply fear of reaching out. They worry so much about how they'll be perceived and whether they'll be rejected that they never act. As a result, they miss out on powerful relationships that could have given them support, insight, inspiration, and more.

Don't let that happen to you. If you're nervous, start with the least intimidating people in your network—friends and career buddies who are at your level. Plan to catch up with each other every few months and exchange notes. That will help you get comfortable with the concept of a personal board of advisors, so over time, you can start to reach further, up the hierarchy and into areas outside your main field. The more you do this, the more your comfort zone will expand, enabling you to eventually build the kind of game-changing board of advisors that top players always have.

As we come to the end of Part III, let's look back on the full picture of what it means to build social agency. When you lack social agency, you feel isolated, misunderstood, and boxed in by other people. Your interactions with others are a constant source of friction and stress in your work life. The more complex your work is, the more you depend on others, and the bigger this burden becomes.

Social agency allows you to turn that whole paradigm on its head. By participating in the agency of others and inviting them to participate in yours, you build relationships with mutual respect and trust. Instead of seeing other people as obstacles, you begin to see them as supporters and collaborators. Interactions that were once frustrating become fulfilling, even joyful. Almost magically, everything is easier and more fun.

The three simple rules you've learned in Part III will ignite this transformation. You don't have to implement them in a specific order, but I tend to think of it as progression. Level 1 of social agency is reverse networking (Rule #5); this is how you build your core relationships. Level 2 is seeking diverse thinking (Rule #6); you start to broaden your circles beyond your comfort zone.

Level 3, the ultimate expression of social agency, is building an advisory board around you. Now you're enlisting the agency of other people to manifest your personal mission, and you have real skin in the game. In the process, you're gaining a greater sense of meaning, new skills, new relationships, and new perspectives—making yourself more valuable and capable than ever in your job.

# VISUAL SUMMARY : BUILD A PERSONAL BOARD OF ADVISORS

### Role Model

- Follow
- Meet once in a while
- Learn through observation

### Coach / Mentor

- Listen
- Meet regularly
- Learn through discussion

### Thought Leader

- Study
- Meet as often as you can
- Learn through debate

### Career Guide

- Explore
- Meet periodically
- Learn through understanding

### Reverse (junior) mentor

- Ask questions
- Meet often
- Learn through questioning

# PART IV
## GROWTH AGENCY

"**Growth agency is the ability to find comfort in the discomfort of learning the new and different.**"

When I first started thinking about what it takes to thrive in modern work, I was primarily focused on personal agency—how to reclaim a sense of control over what you do at work every day. But the more I explored this idea and talked about it with others, the clearer it became that overwhelm, anxiety, and frustration come from multiple places.

Our own personal chaos is one factor; we addressed that with the four rules for personal agency in Part II. Other people are another factor; the three rules for social agency in Part III take care of that. But there was a third theme that kept coming up in conversation after conversation: people worried about whether they were growing fast enough to keep up with the labor market.

It's a legitimate concern. Between automation and AI, it's no longer surprising to see whole categories of business activity transform virtually overnight. If you read management books, you might think the whole world is falling apart. They scare us into thinking that any moment now, all our skills and business models will be disrupted and we'll lose our livelihoods forever. This talk is everywhere, and it generates real anxiety.

You can't get rid of that just by taking control of yourself and your relationships; you also have to take control of your *growth*. You have to continuously develop your professional skills faster than the world around you changes. The question is, how?

---

You can't get rid of that just by taking control of yourself and your relationships; you also have to take control of your *growth*.

---

The mainstream HR answer is to create more training programs and provide the time, resources, and incentives for people to access and learn from those programs. The government of Singapore was arguably the most impressive example of this approach. Their goal was to upskill the entire population of the country, and huge amounts of effort and money went into figuring out what skills would be important, creating the content base, and incentivizing people to participate.

So, of course, when I started thinking about how to foster continuous growth, I looked into the outcomes of that program. When I asked about the top content areas people were consuming, I was expecting to hear things like computer programming or data science— the supposed skills of the future. Actually, the most popular course of all was the Korean language. Why? Because Singaporeans love to watch Korean soap operas.

As it turns out, giving people lots of content and incentives doesn't work that well. It's a viable solution for people who have been laid off; they have time and real motivation to learn. But for the most part, this approach doesn't create a culture of learning. It creates a culture of dabbling—a culture where you'll spend a day consuming content just to get a certificate to put on your LinkedIn profile, without actually acquiring any new skills.

That kind of "learning" doesn't help anyone. I wanted to understand what it took to drive *genuine* continuous learning—the kind of learning my team did when COVID made our old business model impossible. In a span of a few weeks, we acquired the skills to turn that crisis into an opportunity to do better, make more money, and create a bigger impact. And it wasn't just about learning new things; we also had to let go of old things along the way. We had to adapt to a new reality and do it fast.

We did it again on a smaller scale just recently. We were supposed to start a major engagement for one of our largest clients, but it was delayed and it was looking like the whole project might be canceled. We spent about a week trying to salvage the situation, but it was proving more and more difficult. That's when we decided to let go of the original plan and look at other problems that need to be solved. The ability to adapt allowed us to turn a dead deal into a bigger, better project.

That's growth agency. Its power goes beyond simply keeping up with the changing times. When you have high growth agency, change is no longer a threat—it's an opportunity. You don't need to worry about the future because you'll have confidence in your ability to adapt, no matter what happens.

> When you have high growth agency, change is no longer a threat—it's an opportunity.

"With a simple shift in mindset and a few new habits, the pace of your learning will skyrocket."

# 11 | Rule #8: Learn in the Flow of Work

Back in Chapter 2, I talked about the half-life of skills: the amount of time it takes for a learned skill to become irrelevant in the job market. According to my firm's research on this subject, it was around 25 years for technical skills during the 1990s. That means that someone who graduated in that era would have reasonably expected to retrain about once a decade, or maybe less.

By 2020, the half-life of technical skills was more like 4 years. With the advent of generative AI, it's probably even lower—maybe as little as 1 year.

That figure is scary... and it's also a little hard to wrap your head around. It tells us that we'll have to effectively replace all our technical skills every few years, but what exactly does that mean? What kind of effort does that take? How much time do we have to dedicate to learning to keep up with that pace?

The answer turns out to be about 100 days a year.[2] In other words, we have to spend *one third* of our work time learning new things. If "learning" means taking time away from your usual work to do some kind of formal training, this is obviously impossible. That would mean spending 2.5–3 hours *every day* training. Who has that kind of time to spare?

The only way to even come close to this pace of learning is to learn in the *flow* of work. Traditional training interrupts your work; you must stop your normal activities and go learn. Modern learning is baked into your workflow; you're improving your skills and acquiring new ones in the process of doing your job. With a simple shift in mindset and a few new habits, the pace of your learning can skyrocket.

## What Drives Learning?

Before we talk about how to learn in the flow of work, let's address a more basic question: how does learning happen at all? What kinds of activities actually result in meaningful, useful growth?

If you're thinking about anything related to a classroom, think again. According to research by Bob Eichinger (the talent development expert I mentioned back in Chapter 2), a full 25 percent of our learning comes through hardship—making mistakes and overcoming challenges. That's powerful stuff, but unfortunately, we can't orchestrate hardship, so let's look at the other 75 percent of our learning. The vast majority

---

[2] This number comes from research my team did with a client, where we looked at about 20 technical skills across several corporate divisions and measured how long employees took to become a competent novice in a new skill *adjacent to* their current skills. Combine that with the number of skills a person uses and the rate at which those skills lose their relevance, and you find that it takes about 800 hours of learning a year just to keep up. (Note that this is for technical skills, not "soft" skills.) Given the way AI has advanced since we did this study, that figure is probably conservative.

of it—70 percent—comes from practical experience. Another 20 percent comes through learning from others, particularly coaches and mentors. Formal training only accounts for a paltry 10 percent.

And yet, in the world of professional development, the focus is overwhelmingly on training. Leaders and HR professionals spend a huge amount of time thinking about what training to offer, how to make it better, and how to incentivize people to do it... and all the while, training is the LEAST powerful source of learning for the human mind. No wonder it's such a challenge to build training programs that work.

So, if we want to create an environment where learning is inevitable, we have to look at the other two options: experience and other people. For fast-paced, continuous learning that's both effective and sustainable, those are the key vehicles.

For some lucky people, growth on the job happens naturally because their work is designed to be challenging, and they have great mentors to help them meet those challenges. However, you're probably not so fortunate. Your job might feel mundane much of the time—filled with repetitive, rigid tasks. Your superiors probably don't provide thoughtful, timely guidance and feedback. Most of the time, you don't feel like you're growing at all.

That's exactly what I hear all the time: *There's no growth in my job. Everything is prescribed and has to be done exactly according to protocol. There's no room for creativity. I've been doing the same thing the same way for years.*

People who feel this way often look for external solutions. They hope for a promotion or reassignment to a more challenging role, believing there is nothing left to learn in their current position. They might even decide to leave their company in pursuit of perceived growth opportunities elsewhere.

However, the reality is that it's exceedingly rare to find a situation where there is truly *no* room for growth. Even in the most mundane, boring, and rigid jobs, I've seen people who seem to be growing phenomenally, month after month and year after year. Within the constraints of their job, they find ways to keep getting better—and because they keep getting better, the boundaries of their job often expand over time.

Those people have different mindsets. Instead of looking for growth from the outside, they treat every day as an opportunity to learn. It sounds like a cliché, I know, but stay with me. We're going to break down exactly what it looks like to take advantage of the hidden growth opportunities all around you—the five key ways to learn in the flow of work.

## (1) Improve Your Work Product

Every day at work, you're creating some sort of work product. It might be a physical product, a spreadsheet, a dashboard, a report, a presentation, a conversation—*something* that another person uses or consumes in some way. You might even have a few different work products.

If this sounds familiar, that's because it's central to Rule #2: focus on your consumer. As you learned in Chapter 5, spending time with your consumer and understanding their needs is crucial for your personal agency. It prevents you from being pulled in a dozen different directions by all your other bosses and stakeholders, which helps you establish a sense of control over your day-to-day work.

Well, focusing on your consumer is also one of the most effective ways to drive your own growth. When you test your work product with your consumer, they will *tell* you how to make it better. The whole process of refining the work product does double duty as both productive work *and* learning.

As an example, let's consider once again the process of writing this book. I worked diligently with various people before finally having the draft in my hands. So, did the draft capture the core message of the book? Would it grab the attention of the target audience? Did it establish me as a credible and relatable messenger? Was the promised benefit to the reader clear? Did the language strike the right tone?

To answer all these, I had meaningful conversations and feedback sessions with those involved in the process. Parts were polished here and there until the draft had taken shape in the way that mattered to me. I believe the experience for all of us was mutually beneficial. The simple act of asking for feedback generated multiple layers of learning, without interrupting the flow of work at all.

This one thing—creating a feedback loop around your work product—can give you several hours of growth a week. It's one of the most impactful changes I've made in my team and business, leading to creative ideas, efficiency improvements, new skills, and more.

However, there are still those who never do it. For instance, what is the point of a monthly dashboard if, say in 5 years, you never bothered to reach out or ask questions? That's a huge missed opportunity for learning.

## (2) Consume a Lot of Content

When I was growing up and wanted to learn, I had to go to the library and spend hours finding the right books and scanning them for the information I wanted. Now, virtually all of human knowledge is at our fingertips through Google, YouTube, TikTok, and countless other online platforms. Even incredibly complicated things can be learned by watching, listening, and reading the work of others who already know.

That's why I recommend spending about half an hour a day consuming informational content. These 30 minutes are not intended to be super-efficient, targeted learning; treat them as a break from highly intensive work. Go beyond tips and tricks you can use immediately. Take an exploratory, experimental approach. Allow yourself to stumble upon things you never thought you'd be interested in. Dive into topics that are both important *and* intriguing.

In addition to budgeting those 30 minutes a day, make a commitment to talk to someone at least once a week about what you've learned. This is important because when you're consuming information in this way, the growth doesn't necessarily come from the consumption itself. It happens later, in the conversations and applications that make you connect the dots between different ideas. Those connections are always more evident in hindsight, which is why it's crucial to build in time to look back. That reflection is even more powerful when you do it with someone else, who can shine a different light and help you see things you might not notice on your own.

While a certain amount of serendipitous consumption is part of the equation here, just be careful of going down unproductive rabbit holes for too long. There's a lot of nonsense online, so you'll have to learn to judge what's worth your time and what isn't.

## (3) Be Curious About People

Every day, you're moving through the world and bumping into people who spend their time thinking about completely different things than you do. There's a learning opportunity there—a chance to see the world from a different vantage point. You never know who may have something valuable to teach you, but most people let those opportunities walk right by.

For example, several years ago, I went to a wedding in Mumbai. Traditional Indian weddings are famously extravagant, lasting 3 or 4 days with multiple events each day and hundreds of people at each event. Combine that with Mumbai traffic—some of the worst congestion in the world—and you have a recipe for a logistical nightmare.

On the final day of the wedding, I bumped into the wedding planner, and just out of curiosity, I asked her what the craziest thing was that had happened in the last 4 days. She said that the day before, the groom's vehicle got a punctured tire in the middle of the road, an hour away from the venue. I marveled that the groom had arrived only a few minutes late, and she described the three levels of contingency plans that had been in place for exactly that type of emergency. For her, that level of planning was just standard procedure, but I was deeply impressed.

Years later, I was helping a client with their business plan for a risky project, with high potential for multiple things to go wrong. Anxiety around the whole endeavor was running high. That's when I remembered the wedding planner and her multi-level contingency plan, and I decided to do the same thing. Together, the client and I walked through each risk and decided exactly what to do if Plan A went sideways, and then what to do if Plan B went sideways too. By the end of the process, anxiety has turned into confidence and excitement.

All of this is just to say that when you meet other people, it pays to turn up your curiosity. It doesn't take much effort—just ask them about what they do and listen with genuine interest. When you give people that kind of attention, they're usually more than happy to share;

people love to talk about themselves, especially to an appreciative audience. You'll be shocked at what you can learn from a person in 10 or 15 minutes.

Most likely, it won't be something that's directly applicable to the work you do, but that doesn't mean it's not valuable. The human brain is incredibly good at making unexpected connections across different domains; you never know when a seemingly irrelevant idea, story, or piece of information will turn out to be useful. Ultimately, every person you get to know brings you a little more insight into *people*, and what could be more valuable? The better you understand people—how they think, how they communicate, what they care about, what they want— the more success you'll have in *any* role, in *any* kind of work.

## (4) Do Post-Mortems

At the end of every project, sit down with everyone involved and talk about how it went. What worked? What didn't? What would you have done differently, knowing what you know now? What will you do differently in the future?

Experience is still the greatest teacher. However, this doesn't mean every experience automatically generates learning. Experiences can quite easily come and go without leaving any kind of mark if you don't take the time to intentionally reflect on them. When things are going wrong in real time, you're usually too busy solving the immediate problem to think about how to prevent it from happening again. The same is true for things that go well; you usually just take the win and move on without stopping to ask how you can replicate that result next time.

The post-mortem is a crucial step for transforming experience into true learning. By doing it together with your team, you'll collect more insights and come up with better improvements than you would on your own. Plus, you'll get aligned, so you're not the only one trying to do things differently next time.

In my world, the post-mortem is standard practice on almost every team. It's such a low-hanging fruit and it provides so much growth. I love doing it so much that I even sit in on *other* teams' post-mortems to see what I can learn from their experiences.

## (5) Pitch and Fail

If you're an entrepreneur, marketer, or writer, the idea of pitching is very familiar. When you need to get other people on board with your idea, you present it in the clearest, most compelling way possible. If you don't succeed, your idea doesn't get to move forward. You go back to the drawing board to improve upon your initial idea or find a better way to express it.

This sounds like a ruthless and perhaps unappealing process, but it's a powerful driver of learning. People who pitch regularly are constantly having to think deeply about their ideas, see things from their audience's perspective, refine their judgment, try new things, and overcome their fear of failure. If they don't, they won't survive the competition.

However, most people rarely have to pitch. It's not a typical part of the corporate work experience. In fact, most employees don't believe it's their place to offer ideas at all. They assume the answer will always be no.

That may be true, but don't let it stop you. I push my team to constantly pitch ideas to me, even though I know—and they know—that 99 percent of the time, I'll say no. I want to hear their ideas for research projects we could do, tools we could build, programs we could create, and more. More importantly, I want *them* to think creatively about those things, which they probably wouldn't do nearly as much if no one was open to hearing their ideas. It's the practice of pitching that's valuable, much more than the actual ideas that get pitched.

## Conclusion

Learning in the flow of work is the simplest, easiest, most impactful way to cultivate your growth agency. But don't take my word for it—just try these ideas for a week. By Friday, I bet you'll feel like you've grown by leaps and bounds. Your daily work will be more interesting than it was on Monday. Most importantly, you'll see that you don't need to rely on someone else's investment in you to grow. You don't need a promotion, training, or anything other than what's already at your fingertips.

If 1 week makes a noticeable difference, imagine doing this for 6 months. In June, you'll be able to look back at January and see major upgrades in what you're doing and how well you're doing it. That's how you know you can keep up with the rapid pace of change in the modern world.

The best part is that you haven't added a new burden to your workload. All this learning happens within the existing flow of your work. All you have to do is make a few small tweaks to your mindset and habits. Ultimately, curiosity is the key. Give your brain permission to wander, to explore, to ask questions… and you'll find that the opportunities to learn are all around you every day.

Ultimately, curiosity is the key. Give your brain
permission to wander, to explore, to ask
questions. . . and you'll find that the
opportunities to learn are all
around you every day.

# VISUAL SUMMARY : LEARN IN THE FLOW OF WORK

**Learn from Social Media / AI**

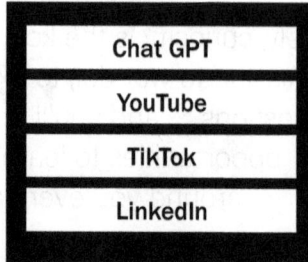

- Chat GPT
- YouTube
- TikTok
- LinkedIn

*30 min*
*4 X*
*week*

**Learn from Work Product**

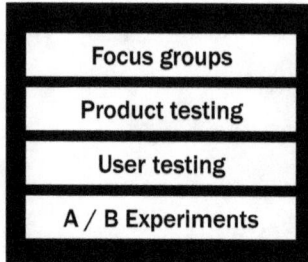

- Focus groups
- Product testing
- User testing
- A / B Experiments

*60 min*
*4 X*
*week*

**10 hours / week**

**Learn from Others / Experts**

- Communities
- Coach / mentor
- Expert talks
- SME Connect

*60 min*
*2 X*
*week*

**Learn from the Team**

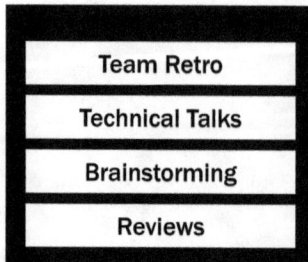

- Team Retro
- Technical Talks
- Brainstorming
- Reviews

*60 min*
*2 X*
*week*

# 12 | Rule #9: Stack Skills to Rise Up

I know someone who started his career in marketing at 22 years old, and now he's the CEO of a food delivery business that operates across six countries. He managed to climb all the way to the very top of the corporate ladder, a feat that very few people ever accomplish. How long did this journey take him?

The traditional path usually takes at least 20 years, if not 30 or more. A marketing guy would have to go deeper and deeper into his field, becoming highly specialized and experienced, to rise through the ranks. Then, if he is identified as a high-potential leader, he might be given the opportunity to do stints in other areas of the company, to round out his capabilities and perspective as an executive. It would be a long, slow process.

This guy did it in *seven years*. That's right—by 29 years old, he was leading an entire business, and not a small one.

This is what's possible in the world of modern work, but *not* if you only focus on deepening your expertise in one area. That's called upskilling, and it's the slow train. If you want to ride the rocket ship, you have to focus on skill *stacking*.

Skill stacking is the strategic combination of different but complementary skills that make you uniquely valuable. In the case of this CEO, he started out in marketing, then acquired skills in customer experience, then data and machine learning, then product innovation, then application development, then AI… and each new skill wasn't just a step forward. It was a giant leap upward in terms of his ability to understand the business as a whole.

Each new skill, instead of simply adding to your value, multiplies it. That's what makes it possible to advance your career two to four times faster than with traditional upskilling. Once you embrace this rule, you'll see opportunities everywhere to grow your skill stack and multiply your value.

## Upskilling Isn't Enough

Google the word "upskilling," and you'll find a huge body of research that's been done on this subject in the last couple of decades. Everyone is talking about upskilling. As soon as digital technology came online and started to accelerate the pace of change, corporations and governments started to worry about how the workforce would keep up. Upskilling was the answer—make sure employees regularly "update" their skills within their area of expertise. According to the World Economic Forum (2025), 60 percent of today's workforce will have to upskill to stay relevant in the years to come.

And that's exactly the problem. Upskilling is necessary to not fall behind, but it's not enough to get you ahead. In the past, before the world began changing so fast, staying stagnant required no learning at all, so if you put some effort into getting better and better at your area of expertise, you could rise above the rest. Now, you're swimming against a constant current of change. That same effort is barely enough to keep you in place. If you try even harder, you will still just be inching ahead.

> Upskilling is necessary to not fall behind,
> but it's not enough to get you ahead.

To make any real progress, you need a totally different strategy. You need something that will lift you right out of that current and let you take a big leap forward. That's what skill stacking does.

Consider it from the perspective of a hiring manager. Let's say I'm in the market to recruit a customer experience person, and a candidate with 2 or 3 years of experience is worth around $80,000-$100,000. A few more years of experience might boost their value by 5 or 10 percent. However, if that person has an additional skill that complements their customer experience capabilities—something like video production, data science, or marketing—I'm willing to pay 30 or 40 percent more to get them on my team. They don't even have to be the best at both of those skills; I'd rather have someone who is above average at two valuable skills than someone who is the absolute greatest at just one.

Why? Think of it in terms of design and production. For any product or service, there are those who create the idea and those who execute it. It typically takes multiple rounds of back-and-forth for those two sides to understand each other and bring the concept to life, and along the way, there's usually some loss of fidelity to the original idea. However, if my designer has production skills, we might be able to skip that back-and-forth altogether. Even if they still have to collaborate with a production team, we'll be able to cut down the number of iterations because the two sides will understand each other better. I can do more and faster with a smaller team; plus, people who can see the business from more than one angle tend to bring more insight and creativity to the table.

The truth is, it's pretty risky these days to put all your eggs in one skill basket, especially if that skill is a technical one. Technology may very well make that skill obsolete sooner or later. For example, Cognitive Labs recently released the world's first AI software engineer, Devin. Not only can it understand instructions but also solve problems, plan a sequence of actions, and execute the plan. It's better than majority of human software engineers out there. Plus, through machine learning, Devin continually gets better at tasks it has never even been explicitly trained to do. If you're a software engineer who specializes in a certain coding language, it's only a matter of months before Devin is better than you. Then what do you do? You'll never be able to upskill as fast as this machine. The only alternative is to stack your skills.

If you've been in the workforce for a long time, this might go against what you've been trained and advised to do. Many people who are in their 40s or older were taught to stick to their lane and become as specialized as possible. Personally, I know that my generation often derived much of their identity and self-value from their expertise in one area.

We can even be snobby and exclusive about our specializations. This culture is often systemic; in most universities in the world, studying across departments is not encouraged. When I was an undergraduate studying engineering, I took one course in English literature and became the butt of jokes in my class.

Contrast that with the liberal arts philosophy, where the goal is not to develop one area of expertise but to develop a keen ability to *think* and *learn* in general. To do that, liberal arts students explore a little of virtually every subject—literature, history, philosophy, art, science, and more. There's a good reason so many CEOs come from a liberal arts background and have done a variety of things over the course of their careers.

Exclusive specialization in one area made sense when the half-life of skills was long. Now, it no longer serves us. So the question becomes, how do you stack skills strategically, so they work together to multiply your value and leapfrog you ahead of the competition?

## Stack Across the Vectors

For a business to succeed in a competitive market, it has to find its niche—the thing it does better than anyone else. In the same way, you need to find *your* niche to succeed in the marketplace of skills. As we've established, becoming more and more expert in a single area is no longer a highly effective way to do this. To be unique, you need to combine two or more things... but which ones?

We're not talking about random combinations here. Look for adjacent skills that are the highest and best use of your learning time. If you're a financial analyst, it makes more sense to learn production skills that will improve the quality of your reports than to learn about climate change. If you're an airline cabin crew member, you'll get more value from studying a foreign language than studying data science. You want to stack skills that complement and strengthen each other, while also expanding your perspective beyond your primary specialty.

One of the best ways to do this is to think back to the vectors of complexity: desirability, feasibility, viability, and sustainability. If you can become reasonably good at three or more, you are probably ready to lead a business.[3] I know startup founders in their 20s who have built that multi-vector proficiency, which has enabled them to build businesses worth $100 million and more. When you can combine all those capabilities, the sky's the limit.

So, looking at these vectors is a good way to map out your skill stack.

| Desirability | Feasibility |
|---|---|
| *(think design school)* user studies, design thinking, user testing... | *(think engineering school)* production, testing, quality assurance... |
| Viability | Sustainability |
| *(think business school)* business modeling, valuation, resource allocation... | *(think psychology/sociology)* impact analysis, mitigation, ethics... |

Start by identifying the vector of your primary area of expertise. Then, look at skills in other vectors that would make you even more effective in your current role.

For example, any kind of creative skill (desirability) combines extremely well with an understanding of data analytics (feasibility/viability). This duo allows you to both generate ideas and use data to test, validate, and sharpen them.

Another great combination is any technical skill (feasibility) with an understanding of business finances (viability). This enables you to

---

[3] Some might argue that the sustainability vector isn't as important as the others. That is becoming less and less true over time. When I started my career, most senior leaders focused primarily on viability. As technology became more integral to business, the feasibility perspective gained more value. With the success of Apple and the consumer movements that followed, desirability gained equal footing. We're now seeing a similar rise in the importance of sustainability.

design technical solutions with financial considerations in mind, which make your solutions far more likely to succeed.

Almost any skill can combine well with automation. If you learn how to design and implement automations, you can multiply your productivity and that of your team, which obviously multiplies your value.

As you think about how to build your skill stack, pay attention to your instincts. Explore the things that capture your interest and imagination; that's a sign that there are probably valuable connections to be made to your existing skills. Plus, you're more likely to develop a meaningful level of skill in something you genuinely enjoy than something that feels forced.

Don't worry too much about being efficient about this, especially early in your career. Remember the liberal arts approach: experiment a little with many things to get a big-picture sense of how it all fits together. If you build the muscle of taking on different types of challenges (and learning to enjoy them) at an early stage of your development, you're much more likely to truly master multiple vectors of complexity. So, in the beginning, allow yourself to take an experimental approach; you can become more selective as your skill stack grows.

## What a Skill Stack Looks Like

Ideally, your combination of skills will create not just a marginal improvement but a *dramatic* one. To understand what I mean by dramatic, consider this recent combination in the business world: Figure1's robotics and OpenAI's generative artificial intelligence. Together, they can create artificial intelligence that *moves*, opening the door to solving an endless array of problems in the physical world.

Here are a few examples of real people who have stacked their skills in ways that created dramatic improvements.

Simon is a highly proficient supply chain professional; he's very good at managing manufacturing, logistics, transportation, procurement, scheduling, etc. Over the last year or so, he started going deeper into automation, with the goal of creating algorithms that could mimic the ways people in his team made decisions. Every time they made a decision—what to do about transportation delays in Yemen, or nickel production problems in Indonesia—he fed the information into the algorithm so it could learn how to emulate that behavior. This person was worth $250,000 before, but his value has doubled in the last year— something he certainly could not have achieved by learning more about supply chain.

Ria is a visual storyteller in the advertising industry; she's highly skilled at generating creative narratives through imagery. On top of that, she invested about a year and a half in learning about brand valuation. Now, when she talks to an executive team about changing the narrative around their brand, she can put a financial value on the benefits. For example, she recently worked with a CEO whose insurance company was associated in consumers' minds with negative things like accidents, illness, and tragedy. She was able to show that if the brand could become associated with positive things like being healthy, living longer, and enjoying life, its value would increase by 20–25 percent. This skill makes her a unique talent in the advertising world.

Jay is a bank executive who went back to school and studied financial algorithms. He used that skill and his network from the banking world to create an investment fund that trades automatically, even while he's sleeping. The algorithm finds opportunities in the market in real time and acts on them without any human interference.

He now works 2 days a month managing $80 million, taking home 2 percent—which is pretty close to what he made as a full-time bank executive.

## Skill Stacking Advice

As you start to build your skill stack, there are a few important things to keep in mind.

### 1. Do *not* dabble.

There is a big difference between skill stacking and dabbling. Skill stacking is mastering multiple skills that complement each other—or at least gaining enough proficiency to apply those skills in a meaningful way. Dabbling is skimming the surface in a way that doesn't build any real capabilities.

That's one of the most dangerous things you can do in today's market. It's a waste of time and effort, and with the pace of change we're all facing, there's no time to lose. When you decide to explore a new skill, do it with the full intention to become good, if not great, at actually using the skill in a practical way.

### 2. Start now.

The sooner you start building your skill stack, the better. You might think you're too young and should focus on your primary area first. On the flip side, you might think you're too old, and it's too late for this to make a difference for you. Forget about both of those self-limiting ideas. The best time to start was on day one of your career; the second-best time to start is now.

> The best time to start was on day one of your career; the second-best time to start is now.

The longer you wait, the more you disadvantage yourself. Skill stacking takes time—you won't gain meaningful proficiency in a new area overnight. As you age, fluid intelligence (the ability to think flexibly) tends to go down while crystallized intelligence (the accumulation of knowledge) goes up. Fluid intelligence makes it easier to learn new things, so it's a good idea to start skill stacking as early as possible.

### 3. Take mentoring with a grain of salt.

As we transition from the traditional work paradigm to the modern one, mentoring can be a double-edged sword. What worked in the past is no longer necessarily good advice. If you're young, carefully consider the advice you get from older mentors. They certainly may have valuable wisdom, but they may also share advice that's based on what worked for *them*, not what works *now*. If a mentor discourages you from exploring areas outside your specialty, recognize that they might not be the best authority on how to succeed in modern work.

### 4. As a leader, be open.

On the flipside of this, if you're a leader, manager, or mentor, be open to employees who want to grow outside the traditional boundaries. If you're steeped in the traditional paradigm, it may seem like a waste of time and money for a designer to learn about financial modeling or a procurement expert to explore AI. Hopefully, by now, you can see that these kinds of skill combinations not only benefit the team and the company; they allow you to do more with fewer people and bring fresh insight to the business as a whole.

## Conclusion

A few years ago, the idea of a billion-dollar company with less than ten people sounded crazy. I thought it was insane; from what I had seen in my career, it took 10,000 people to run a company of that size. There was simply no business model that would enable so few people to generate so much revenue.

But the reality is, it's already happening. So much of what a company traditionally does can now be digitized, automated, and/or outsourced. When production, distribution, and even customer support no longer require significant resources, what is left? Just a few key capabilities: ideation, design, marketing, and business management. With the right skill stacks and AI tools, it's no longer a stretch to think that ten people can cover those areas, even for a global company with millions of customers.

Obviously, not all companies will be so extreme. But the trend here is that the value of a company per employee is headed up; fewer people are required to produce the same result. To stay competitive, companies will *need* multi-skilled employees. If you specialize in just one skill, organizations would rather buy your skill as a service than give you a full-time job. In the world of modern work, if you want to stay valuable, you've got to stack your skills.

> In the world of modern work, if you want to stay valuable, you've got to stack your skills.

# VISUAL SUMMARY : STACK SKILLS TO RISE UP

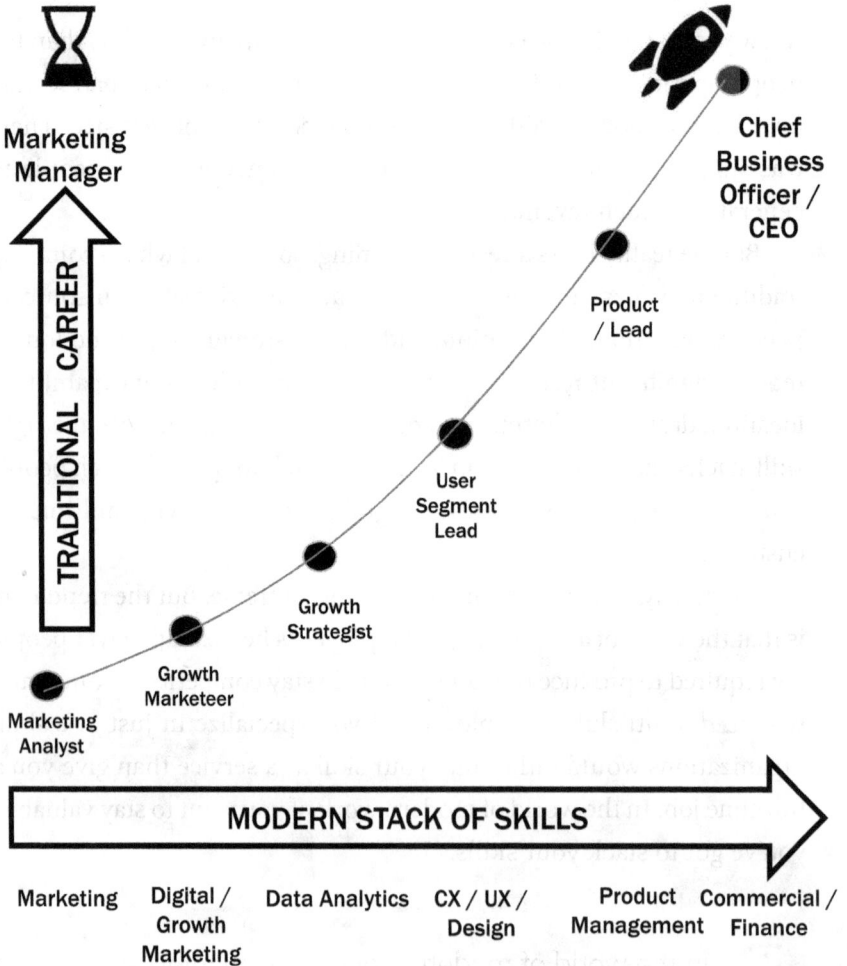

Marketing
Manager

TRADITIONAL CAREER

Chief
Business
Officer /
CEO

Product
/ Lead

User
Segment
Lead

Growth
Strategist

Growth
Marketeer

Marketing
Analyst

## MODERN STACK OF SKILLS

Marketing    Digital /
          Growth     Data Analytics    CX / UX /
          Marketing                 Design    Product    Commercial /
                                                     Management    Finance

# 13 | Rule #10: Run a Side Hustle

S o, here we are. The final rule.

To be honest, this rule is by far the most powerful and the most challenging at the same time. The highest agency individuals I have encountered in life have multiple side hustles that live alongside their main life of work.

When my wife and I had our first child, she decided to leave her work as a mathematician and financial analyst to be a full-time parent. Then, when our son graduated from high school in 2019, she wanted to start working again. We both knew that because of her extended break from her career, going into the job market would probably mean doing something she was overqualified for, where she would report to someone who was less intelligent and experienced than her—a surefire recipe for frustration.

If she wasn't going to find the work she wanted through the job market, we would have to create it ourselves. That meant starting our own business. So, we asked ourselves:

> If resources were no object, what problem
> would we want to solve?

This was a question I had never entertained before. As a company man, I never felt it was my place to ask. Up until this point, my professional life was 100 percent focused on doing well at work and building strong businesses there. I wasn't sure where to begin.

My wife was, though. She wanted to help the hundreds of millions of kids—especially in underdeveloped countries—who didn't get high-quality education and never had the guidance to truly develop their abilities. So often, they don't even know about the opportunities that might be available to them, much less have the skills or confidence to access those opportunities. There was no algorithm to help disadvantaged young people discover their talents and find programs, scholarships, jobs, and other opportunities to match.

So, we said, "Why don't we build that algorithm?" I had created similar tools for executive recruiting, and we could apply the same principles and skills to this use case. My wife founded the company and won a grant from the Singapore government to start building the platform. I became an active investor, guiding the development of algorithms for identifying a person's life skills and matching those skills with potential career areas.

> This is my side hustle, and in building it
> over the last 5 years, it has built me.

It has created a level of growth agency I never thought could even exist. It has centered my perspective, changed my mindset and beliefs, developed my confidence, broadened my network, diversified my skills, and fueled my passion.

That's why you should always strive to run a side hustle—in other words, to invest your time and energy in something outside of work that's more than just a hobby. I know, it sounds crazy. How on earth can you be expected to add a whole other project to your life when you're already overwhelmed at work? (Not to mention, you might have a family to take care of, too.)

If you're skeptical—which is totally fair—bear with me.

I promise, the idea behind running a side hustle is *not* to exhaust you even further. It's the opposite—to make you feel *more* energized, capable, and confident than ever before, both at work and outside of it.

## The Opposite of a Distraction

Traditionally, anything outside of work is considered a distraction from your career. Many companies have policies in place that actively discourage or even prohibit you from doing paid work or running a business outside of your full-time job. Even if those activities are completely unrelated to what your company does and therefore are not a competitive threat, traditional management thinking says they're stealing the attention and energy you should be dedicating to your job.

In the world of modern work, this idea flips on its head for several reasons.

The first is simply the proliferation of side hustles. There are so many more ways to run your own business today than there were

10 years ago. Many young people today already have a side hustle before they even graduate from school or get their first formal job. It's becoming more and more common to have multiple work activities and multiple income streams.

But there's another important reason for rethinking the orthodoxy on side hustles: focusing too hard on one thing can actually *contribute* to burnout. If your job is the one thing that dominates your life, you'll have a hard time turning your mind away from it even when you're not actively engaged in it. That kind of obsessive rumination does nothing good for your mental or emotional state.

You *need* an opportunity to turn your attention to something else—ideally, something that lights you up. Something you're passionate about. Something that matters to you. Something that challenges you in a different way than work does. That's what a side hustle is for.

You might be wondering, can't raising a family or pursuing a hobby do the same thing? Why does it have to be a side hustle? And what exactly *is* a side hustle anyway?

## Four Elements of a Side Hustle

I'm so glad you asked—I've been contemplating those questions for years. Through my research and my personal experience, I've found that for the purposes of this rule, there are four key elements that make a good side hustle. The combination of these four elements is what unlocks the ultimate level of growth agency we're aiming for here.

### (1) Passion

A side hustle must be something you're passionate about. We talked about passion in the context of Rule #1: Bring your own motivation.

While it's crucial to find some aspect of your work you can get excited about, the reality for most people is that their work doesn't line up with their greatest passions in life. In fact, one study (Hagel et al., 2017) reported that only 13 percent of corporate employees actually believe they're passionate about what they do (which probably doesn't surprise you—it certainly didn't surprise me).

That's why an essential element of a good side hustle is *choice*. You get to decide what your mission is. Just the fact that you're at the steering wheel will trigger a sense of agency, and that sense gets amplified when you choose something that naturally gets you fired up. It should be something you enjoy doing regardless of any external reward— something you would happily spend your evenings and weekends on, something you can talk about for hours to anyone who will listen.

The one pitfall to beware of here is choosing something you think you *should* do but that doesn't really light you up. It sounds obvious, but this is a surprisingly common mistake, especially among conscientious and ambitious people. No matter how hard you try to turn a "should" into a real passion, it will eventually start to feel like a burden. Needless to say, that's the opposite of what we're trying to achieve here.

I know—so far, this sounds no different from a hobby. So, let's look at the other three elements of a good side hustle.

## (2) Value

A hobby becomes a side hustle when you start creating value for others. This can be material value—as in a business where you exchange products or services for money—and it can also be social value. More often than not, the two go together.

In fact, I would argue that you should aim for both. Pursuing financial value alone—for example, by trading cryptocurrency—won't create growth agency. Even if you're passionate about crypto, and even if you're sharing the financial benefit with others, that kind of activity doesn't require you to participate in anyone else's agency, or you in theirs.

However, focusing exclusively on social impact isn't ideal either; there's a real benefit to thinking about profit as well. It disciplines your thinking and challenges you to build something that's financially viable and sustainable—in other words, something that's made to last. It requires you to invest something more than just your time—to take a risk, to have skin in the game. Having something material at stake elevates the whole endeavor and pushes you to grow in ways you wouldn't otherwise.

For example, I have a friend who loves rock climbing and has been doing it as a hobby for many years. She realized that there's a particular kind of chalk that was extremely effective for improving her grip, but it was hard to find in her part of the world. So, she partnered with her preferred chalk company to start a franchise and bring the product to more rock climbers like her. She found a way to turn her passion into a business that not only makes money but also makes a positive difference for the rock-climbing community.

Another person I know helps run a nonprofit organization that uses "waste" food from grocery stores—perfectly good food that's going to be thrown away—to help feed children in schools. This is an interesting case because there's no literal profit involved. However, the organization does have to sustain itself financially, and that's a major concern for this person. Compare that to simply volunteering in a food bank every week, where it's not your job to worry about keeping the organization alive. That responsibility adds a new dimension to the activity and transforms it from a hobby into a serious side hustle.

Why is it a good thing to take on all this responsibility? Because you can't shoulder the burden on your own, and that's the whole point. As you're about to see, growth agency becomes both a requirement and an inevitable outcome of running your side hustle.

## (3) Skills

When you're part of a big organization (as you are at work), when challenges come up that aren't in your area of specialty, you can always say, "Not my problem." But in your side hustle, *everything* is your problem. You have little choice but to expand your skills to solve those problems… and suddenly, you realize you're capable of so much more than you thought.

You also realize you don't have time to take a formal course on every skill you need to learn. So, how can you acquire those skills faster? By reaching out to people you know who already have them. Tap the experts around you to learn just enough to move forward. This is a powerful way to build your growth muscles, and it's even more important in a side hustle than a full-time startup situation because there's less time available. You only have nights and weekends to work on this, so you must be as efficient as possible.

For example, in my side hustle, we had figured out the "personal strengths" side of the algorithm, and the next big jump was to match those strengths with undergraduate programs around the world. If I tried to solve that problem inside my consulting firm, it would probably take 6–8 months and a significant budget to create the database. But we started asking around among our contacts at universities, and it ended up only taking 2 months. With help from the right people, we became capable of far more than we had expected.

The skills you learn for your side hustle will only add to your value at work. As you'll learn in Part IV of this book, adding adjacent and complementary skills is the most powerful way to accelerate your career in the world of modern work (as opposed to traditional work, where linear growth in one specialty was preferred). Once you've learned how to acquire skills quickly for your side hustle, you'll be able to apply that same accelerated learning approach to new skills at work. In short, your side hustle makes you grow, *and* it makes you better at growing.

> In short, your side hustle makes you grow,
> *and* it makes you better at growing.

## (4) People

In your side hustle, you won't just need other people's knowledge—you'll need their time and effort too. When you're running a business or even a nonprofit, there's always far more to do than you can possibly handle by yourself. However, you'll probably be using your savings or personal income to get started, at least at first, and you can't afford to spend a lot of money. So, how do you enlist other people to help you for free?

Through social agency: you have to participate in other people's agency, then invite them to participate in yours. Running around begging for favors won't work; you might get a few people to pitch in temporarily, but not in any kind of long-term or sustainable way. The only way to get people truly involved and keep them engaged is to build a relationship of mutual trust and respect so they genuinely *want* to help you.

Building these relationships for your side hustle will expand your network in hugely productive and often unexpected ways. Your side hustle is probably pretty different from your work activities, which means it will put you in contact with different kinds of people, increasing the diversity of your social circles. That gives you access to a whole new set of ideas and opportunities, which can spark your creativity and lead you in directions you never would have predicted. It also helps reinforce your practice of Rule #6, which makes you a more skilled collaborator both in your side hustle and at work.

## Conclusion

A side hustle should fuel your passion, create value for you and for others, expand your skills, and build relationships with new people. There are lots of hobbies and gigs that don't have all these elements, and while those activities might spark joy or make money, they won't actually help you thrive at work.

That's the whole goal here, after all. A proper side hustle will energize you, give you confidence, put a smile on your face, and diminish the emotional toll of the drama and frustration at the office. It will make you calmer and more mature in the face of a work crisis, because you will have faced and handled your own crises. It will multiply your productivity, engagement, and confidence at work. It will give you a sense that anything is possible... and you can bring all that positive energy to your job.

That's what I mean when I say my side hustle built me. The person I am now professionally—with my clients, my team, and my peers—is informed by the experience of building this platform with my wife. I could never have had that same experience in a corporate setup; I wouldn't have been the one choosing the problem, enlisting people, building skills, and driving the pursuit of both financial and social value.

Until you've experienced this, you will think it's exhausting. But done right, it's surprisingly not.

Just take this book, for example. It's another side hustle of mine. Despite the grueling tasks and tight deadlines, I powered through because I'm passionate about the message I'm sharing. I'm aiming for both a financial return AND a positive impact on my readers' lives. I'm learning how to write and publish a book (a first for me!), and I'm building new, collaborative relationships to make it all happen.

# VISUAL SUMMARY : RUN A SIDE HUSTLE

**PASSION**

Focus on a domain that is a passion for you

**SKILL**

Leverage your full range of skills, build or borrow the skills you don't have

**PEOPLE**

Learn to attract and enrol the right people to your mission

**VALUE**

Find a way to create tangible value (commercial or social) from the mission

# PART V

## HIGH-AGENCY ORGANIZATIONS

"You can be a high-performance but low-agency organization when uncertainty in your market is low. When uncertainty peaks, however, the only path to performance is through agency."

As I explained at the beginning of this book, the ten rules of agency are intentionally designed for individual people. They can be used by anyone, in any role, in any organization, in any part of the world. Employees no longer have to wait around hoping their environment will change—they can reclaim a sense of control, efficacy, and peace at work all on their own.

However, *organizations* can also use agency to their advantage, as a lever for productivity, growth, and effectiveness. Leaders have the opportunity to design and run their organizations in a way that works for everyone—not just shareholders and customers but also the employees who make it all happen. They hold enormous power in their hands to nurture agency across the organization, and there are massive benefits to be gained by doing so. In fact, encouraging agency is among the lowest-cost, highest-ROI investments an organization can make.

In reality, the *lack* of agency is already a major invisible cost in most organizations. We all know that as individuals, we don't do our best work when we're overwhelmed, anxious, and frustrated. As one study showed, 70 percent of managers feel burnt out (The Adecco Group, 2021); you can imagine how far their companies must be from peak performance.

When organizations notice those lackluster results, the typical response is to dial up the pressure. Traditional management logic says that to increase productivity, you have to raise expectations and increase positive and negative incentives for people to meet those expectations. This is the go-to move, especially in tough economic cycles. Unsurprisingly, it amplifies the overwhelm, frustration, and anxiety for everyone.

An optimist might argue that as economic conditions improve, pressure and stress will go down. On this, I am not an optimist. Even in this current down cycle, there are still pockets of extreme growth and success—for example, in banking, where profits are higher than ever. Following the logic of the optimist, people who work in banking should feel better than people in other sectors... but they don't. What we're dealing with here is not a cyclical problem; it's a fundamental one.

Many leaders are well aware of this. All the CEOs I work with recognize that complexity is rising, the pace of change is accelerating, and hybrid work is complicating the whole mess. They're frustrated by the wasted energy and effort that have become a feature of today's work environment. They want to unlock positive energy and motivate people, but the tools that used to work for this—incentives, communication, corporate policies—aren't working anymore. Their workforce isn't responding to the call to step up, and they don't know why.

*Agency* is the key missing component. Most organizations don't understand this concept, and as a result, they aren't leveraging it. Instead, they keep trying the same old, ineffective solutions and hoping for different results. This is especially interesting because agency is free to use and virtually limitless. Without spending a penny more on incentives, the best teams can multiply their results by 10 or 20 times... and be *happier* at the same time.

To give just one example, consider a global bank I recently worked with. Their typical process to create a 90-day plan is incredibly onerous; to get about a hundred leaders in different business areas to arrive at a consensus takes about a month. Even if there's no bad actor in the game, there's a traffic jam of decisions. Someone has to play the role of referee, decide the criteria of what's important and what's not. There's an endless parade of spreadsheets, documents, and presentations. They have to do this every quarter, so planning becomes a permanent machine that eats up at least 2 percent of revenue (a massive number) and generates untold frustration for the people involved.

My team met with this group of leaders for 1 day, taught them about agency, and within 8 hours, they had a clear 90-day plan. At the beginning of the day, they had 65 initiatives in their plan, and the CEO laughed when I told him my target was 16. In the end, the group got it down to 14. This 1-day investment in agency probably saved *at least* 1 percent of total revenue.

Given these incredible possibilities, why *wouldn't* a company make an effort to increase the agency of its employees? The short answer is they don't know how... which is the reason for Part V of this book.

To fully unlock agency in an organization requires efforts at three levels: the CEO, team leaders, and HR leaders. The CEO sets the example and dedicates the resources to drive the cultivation of agency. Team leaders are the central players who develop agency in their employees. HR leaders provide the training and coaching to support team leaders in that crucial role.

What you'll see in the following chapters is that cultivating agency across a large group of people is *not* the same as motivating them. This is not about getting up on a stage and inspiring hope—that kind of energy is short-lived. This is about quietly building confidence over the long term.

That's a good thing—it means you don't need to be a charismatic leader to unlock agency across your organization. You just need to make a few key shifts in your attention and resources.

"To fully understand agency, it's not enough to develop it in yourself; you also need to cultivate it in your team."

# 14 | For CEOs

The CEO's role in cultivating agency across the organization is simple: set the intention, lead by example, and support everyone else to follow suit.

For agency to become self-sustaining, it has to be more than just a company policy or common practice. It has to be a feature of the culture—a core value. And as all leaders know, culture begins at the top. That's why—although CEOs won't be the ones directly coaching their employees to exercise agency—we're going to focus on them first.

If you're a CEO, you have to do three things to fulfill this role: (1) understand what agency is and how it works, (2) cultivate your own agency, and (3) help your executive team cultivate their agency. In other words, you have to go through the process first-hand. Otherwise, you won't understand what kind of coaching and support your employees will need as *they* go through the process.

You've just spent the last ten chapters on step one. Now, let's focus on steps two and three.

## Cultivate Your Own Agency

You might expect that CEOs have pretty high agency compared to other people, and for the most part, you would be right. Most CEOs have a high level of personal agency—that so-called boardroom confidence (sometimes *over*confidence). It's probably part of the reason they reach the office of CEO.

Good CEOs typically have high growth agency as well. They're always curious, always learning, always aiming to improve. They consume a lot of information, have a variety of skills, and consult frequently with expert advisors. That's pretty standard practice for ambitious, driven leaders who have made it all the way to the top.

However, social agency is often a weak point. There's often a tendency toward a hero mindset: "I'll solve everything myself." Friction with the executive team is often a major source of stress for CEOs—not to mention tensions with the board of directors and shareholders.

So, even if you're a CEO, chances are good that you have some areas to work on where your agency is concerned. Start by answering the seven questions of the Thrive Index, which will tell you how well you're doing overall. Then, do an honest assessment of your practice of each of the ten rules. Some of them are probably already part of your routine; others you might not be doing at all.

This is your baseline. If you're already scoring above 50 on the Thrive Index and actively practicing all 10 rules, congratulations! Keep doing what you're doing.

If not, you have your work cut out for you. Don't try to tackle every weak spot at once, though. Progress tends to be more sustainable when it happens one step at a time. Pick one rule to focus on for at least the next 3 months. Practice it until it feels like a comfortable habit, *then* shift your focus to the next thing. Be sure to take the Thrive Index at least once every 6 months to track your progress.

It's important to point out that because CEOs have high agency, they often struggle to empathize with people who don't. For example, during a recent town hall at a client company, an employee spoke up to express that they were feeling a lot of stress. The CEO's response was basically that we all have stress, and everyone just needs to suck it up and deal with it. Elon Musk is perhaps the most extreme example of this attitude; he demands that his own level of intensity, initiative, and obsession be reflected in everyone around him. He has no patience for anyone who fails to live up to that standard.

That's actually a pretty common mindset. CEOs often assume that high agency is normal, and people who don't have it are less capable, less deserving, and less valuable. They particularly criticize the young generations for their apparent lack of drive and work ethic. They often get frustrated and waste huge amounts of time and energy trying to motivate their people or find better talent.

What these leaders don't realize is that those people have the potential for agency—they just might not be bringing it to work. The same person can have different levels of agency in different environments. A teenage athlete might have remarkably high agency on the football field but not in math class. A middle-aged accountant might have high agency as a parent but not as an employee. Everyone has agency in *some* realm of their life; the question is how you can help them translate that to their work.

Jumping to conclusions and labeling people as capable or incapable of agency—even behind closed doors—is extremely toxic. As you cultivate your awareness of your own agency, take the opportunity to reflect on where it comes from. Sure, you probably have some level of natural tendency toward high agency. But you also had plenty of opportunities, mentors, and life experiences that led you to develop the confidence and the courage to take charge. Resist the urge to judge others for not having those same experiences; your job now is to provide them.

## Develop Your Executives' Agency

To fully understand agency, it's not enough to develop it in yourself; you also need to cultivate it in your team. As they say, you don't fully know something until you teach it. More importantly, this puts you in the same position your team leaders will be in. They're the key drivers of agency on the ground. If you don't tackle the challenge of nurturing agency in your own team, you won't understand the challenge your team leaders face, and you won't be able to give them the support they need to succeed. So, treat your direct reports as your team and start nurturing their agency.

When I suggest this to CEOs, I often meet major resistance. They'll say something like, "These people get paid too much for me to handhold them like that." There's an assumption that senior executives should already have high agency. After all, they have ownership over their domain.

In reality, agency decreases quite rapidly in the organizational chart. Few jobs are designed for high agency—not even the ones near the top. If the buck stops with the CEO, it doesn't stop anywhere else. Plus, there's so much interdependence across functions that executives often feel they're not really in charge of their results; too many other parts of the organization play a role. The more siloed the organization is, the worse this problem becomes. At one of the multinational banks I work with, there are more than 200 senior leaders with "global" in their title. The organization has been sliced so finely that each of those people feels very little control over their outcomes. They're responsible for making big decisions, and yet they often lead low-agency lives.

So, as a CEO, it's not safe to assume that your executive team's agency is already as high as yours. You need to take the time to figure out where each member of the team is starting from. I keep using the word "cultivate" in relation to agency, and I mean it—this is gardening, starting in your backyard. This is how you lead by example.

> I keep using the word "cultivate" in relation to agency, and I mean it—this is gardening, starting in your backyard. This is how you lead by example.

In this process, measurement matters. Judging someone's agency by intuition and casual conversations won't give you the full picture. The Thrive Index is an important starting point, but even that isn't enough to fully understand how to coach a person around agency. You'll need to have in-depth, one-on-one conversations with each member of your team.

Most CEOs already have regular conversations with their senior leaders, but they tend to focus on performance, results, and problem-solving. Occasionally, they might discuss the person's career trajectory in the company. That's about as deep and personal as these conversations usually get.

To help a person cultivate agency, you'll have to go beyond that. The goal is to fully understand where the person is with each of the seven elements in the Thrive Index. This may lead you outside of the "professional" box, into topics like family and mental health. It requires a level of openness and vulnerability that many people aren't accustomed to having in a work context, if at all.

Part of this openness is being willing to talk about what gives *you* purpose and energy. By speaking honestly from the heart, you open the door for the other person to do the same. This helps create a psychologically safe environment, where they can be candid about the ways they might be struggling at work.

Another part of this openness is being willing to accept that other people may get their purpose and energy from something besides the company's mission. CEOs often struggle to accept that, especially from their senior executives. This is particularly true of startup founders. It can feel like a betrayal, or at least a disappointment. But taking these things personally doesn't help anyone—not you, and not your team. The purpose of this conversation is to help the other person maximize their agency, and they can't do that unless they get honest with themselves about what moves them. You don't need to get them to rally around *your* mission; you need to help them identify *their* mission.

Sometimes, you'll end up unlocking unexpected things—and maybe even losing some people. I once had a team member who was succeeding as a consultant but didn't seem fully satisfied with the work. I found out that he grew up in a very religious family, and it had been his childhood dream to become a Catholic priest… and shortly thereafter, he left the team to do exactly that. In another conversation with a struggling team member, it became clear that his sense of purpose was around climate change; he soon left to go work for the United Nations. When another team member revealed that she was going through a difficult life stage and needed a change in context, she ended up transferring to a different role in another country.

Facing the possibility of losing people can be hard when you depend on them for your team's success. Embrace the uncertainty. You cannot control the outcome. The one thing you can control is the trust you build with that person, which paves the way for you to maximize their agency. If the byproduct of that process is that the person leaves your team, that's the best result for everyone in the long run. If you're unwilling to face this risk, you're going to have a hard time unlocking agency.

## Promote a Culture of Agency

Last year, I was invited to a leadership training program at West Point, the most elite academy of the United States military. My first instinct was to pass on the offer. I wasn't sure they had anything valuable to teach me—in my mind, the military was the realm of strict hierarchies and top-down leadership, and the business world I lived in was moving more and more in the opposite direction. In the end, I went anyway, not expecting to get much out of it.

I was surprised when the instructors—all fantastically accomplished military leaders—started to talk about something that sounded a lot like agency. Military operations typically involve both high stakes and high uncertainty. As they say, no plan survives first contact with the enemy; once the action begins, the situation can change in an instant, and there often isn't time to communicate up and down the chain of command. In those moments, soldiers on the ground have to be trained and empowered to make autonomous decisions using their best judgment. If they don't, the plan can't adjust to the reality of the situation, and bad things happen.

To make this work, military leaders distinguish between three different layers of decisions: what, why, and how. The top brass are responsible for articulating *what* the mission is and *why* it's important; the *how* is ultimately up to the operating commander on the ground.

West Point calls this philosophy "decentralized execution." I call it a culture of agency.

It sounds simple and obvious, but most business leaders don't operate this way. They tend to think that "empowering" others to make decisions means letting them decide the what and the why as well as the how. Leaders know that doesn't work—the troops don't have the information, perspective, or skills to make the right call on what and why. So they default to dictating everything, including the how... and that's precisely what makes the team lose agency.

To create a culture of agency, everyone in your organization has to start making this distinction between the what, the why, and the how. Leaders need to understand that it's their role not only to decide the what and why but also to *communicate* the what and why clearly to the troops on the ground; without that information, the troops can't make good decisions about the how. Leaders also need to encourage their troops to make those decisions and train them to do it well. As CEO, you're the seed of this culture.

I say "everyone" needs to start thinking this way, but the reality is there will be resistance at first. Because of that, it's actually not a great idea to push the concept of agency on everyone all at once. If you do, you'll probably get a lot of nods and smiles to your face, followed by shrugs and eye rolls behind your back. It's human nature to be skeptical, and some people may have been punished, sidelined, or disrespected for showing agency in the past. To get them on board, they'll need to see it work in practice.

So, roll out the concept of agency with a small group—maybe ten percent of your workforce—who are working on something mission-critical. Create a high-agency environment within that team. Once that group demonstrates that this approach creates both great results for the business and great well-being for employees, it becomes much easier to break the skepticism barrier with everyone else.

## Conclusion

When you cultivate your own agency *and* the agency of your team, the job of CEO becomes much easier. I don't hold the title of CEO, but I am the leader of my business so I know this firsthand. Now that I'm running a high-agency team, there are times in my team meetings when I don't even have to open my mouth for 20 minutes because other people are driving the conversation with their passion. I just sit back and watch the magic happen.

This whole process is much easier if you're authentic, trustworthy, open about your own challenges, and willing to hold yourself accountable to the same standards as your team. This is easier in some cultural contexts than others. In an open culture that's more egalitarian and accepting of emotional expression, it won't be too difficult. In a highly hierarchical, emotionally distant culture, it will require more effort. I've spent most of my career in Asia, which falls into the latter camp, and I've often seen people work together for 20 years and never really open up to each other. There's a certain formality to these relationships. That doesn't mean openness is impossible; you just may have to try a few times.

That said, you don't need to (and indeed, shouldn't) become the team psychologist. The goal here is simply to enhance each person's sense of agency at work—to make incremental progress relative to where they're starting. If they're starting at 10 percent agency and you help them get to 20 or 30 percent, that's a win. If they're starting at 70 percent, you can aim even higher. Every gain for them is a benefit to you and your organization.

Notice that none of what we've discussed in this chapter depends on your ability to be charismatic. You don't need to have a loud personality or charming demeanor. You don't have to stand on a podium and make rah-rah speeches. You just have to make a commitment to practicing, valuing, and teaching agency.

Through this process of maximizing your own agency, nurturing your executives' agency, and making agency a priority for everyone, you can fundamentally transform your organization. The CEO's personal buy-in and investment in agency is especially important in the early stages, when the concept is new to everyone else. As you'll see in the next chapter, when your team leaders begin to follow your example, they will become the primary drivers of agency throughout the organization. However, it will always be up to the CEO to ensure that agency remains enshrined in the culture.

# 15 | For Team Leaders

W hen it comes to cultivating agency across an organization, team leaders are at the center of it all. By team leaders, I mean the people who are in charge of groups of individual contributors; they might be called managers, supervisors, or some other title. Sometimes it's a formal role, and sometimes it's not.

If this is you, I have great news: you have the greatest power to spread agency. You also have the most to gain from doing so. However, at the same time, team leaders also tend to have the lowest agency of anyone in the organization.

That's why it's crucial for team leaders to pay special attention to agency—and for CEOs and HR leaders to help them. First, you'll need to cultivate your own agency and get the support to keep that agency high over the long term. Then, you'll need to understand the benefits of developing your team members' agency and how to go about doing that. This is the key to fully spreading agency throughout the organization; when team leaders have high agency, it opens the door for everyone else to follow.

## The Central Players

Take a step back and ask yourself: how many teams are in your organization?

As it turns out, this is not a simple question. Every organization knows how many employees they have, as well as how many departments, offices, and regions. Among their employees, they know the breakdowns by gender, race, age, job role, and many other factors. However, when I ask how many teams they have, they stutter and stammer. This is the first mindset shift: the top brass have to start thinking about the organization in terms of teams. Let's explore why.

The traditional playbook of a team leader is focused on managing activities and outcomes. Some team leaders are highly results-oriented and don't care about the details of the activities. Others (often labeled as micromanagers) are actively involved in deciding how things get done. Great managers (which are relatively rare) also recognize that the well-being of the team is important, and they invest time and effort to create harmony, engagement, motivation, and high morale.

However, most team leaders are *not* focused on unlocking agency. In fact, there's quite a lot of fear around agency. Team leaders often believe that if everyone has high agency, the team will become unmanageable and descend into chaos. It's an instinctive concern. If you're aiming for harmony, compliance, and order, and you imagine a world where every member of your team has a mind of their own, initiative, confidence, and opinions... of course you'll worry about losing control.

This is why it's so useful for the top leadership to think about the organization at the team level. From the C-suite, the benefits of agency and the path to cultivate it seem obvious. However, from the perspective of a team leader, we come up against a deep-seated instinct to *resist* agency.

This is problematic since team leaders are poised to become ever more critical to the smooth functioning of organizations. As we continue to develop better and better technology—especially in automation, AI, and robotics—the number of management layers required in an organization will decrease. It will come down to essentially three levels of work: practitioners, team leaders, and executives. Team leaders are the glue that holds the organization together. The better they function, the better the organization will function.

The good news is that agency makes a team leader's job *easier*. Your biggest struggles don't stem from individual practitioners not knowing how to do their work. They come from *people* issues: interpersonal conflicts, politics, and problematic behaviors. A high-agency team will solve 80 to 90 percent of those problems themselves, without escalating to the team leader. They'll have each other's backs. They'll be more aligned. They'll resolve conflicts in a constructive way. All this will lead to more creativity and better ideas, as well as more stability in the team.

I know this firsthand from leading my own team. When I'm struggling with difficult dynamics in the team, I go for a late night run and then sit down somewhere and write my thoughts on my phone. I have a long journal of these notes on team dynamics, stretching back many years... but since I started cultivating agency in my team, those notes have all but stopped.

Team turnover has also gone way down. It's not zero, but it's much lower, and when people do leave, it never comes as a surprise. I see it coming because I'm having open conversations with everyone about what they really want and how they're feeling at work. Occasionally, we'll even get a returnee—someone who leaves to try something else, then decides to come back.

That's a testament to the quality of the experience my team members have at work. They know that here, they're not just resources for getting things done. They are seen and valued as full human beings, and they get to exercise their agency to a greater degree than they could anywhere else.

## Cultivating Team Leader Agency

To cultivate your own agency as a team leader, follow the same basic process I laid out for CEOs in the previous chapter. First, measure yourself on the Thrive Index. Then, do an honest assessment of where you stand with each of the ten rules of agency.

The first few rules in particular pose some deep and challenging questions. What is your purpose? What are you trying to accomplish? What are your superpowers? What are your blind spots? Who are your users? What value are you creating for them? What are your aspirations? What habitual actions will take you in that direction? When I work with team leaders on this—most of whom have at least 8 years of experience—they almost always tell me it's the first time they've reflected on these things.

This reflection process is hugely beneficial, particularly because team leaders often have the lowest agency of anyone in the organization. You might find this surprising; shouldn't the most junior people have the lowest agency? The problem is that team leaders are sandwiched between their bosses and their teams. You have more people to answer to than anyone else, and so the last person you actually answer to is yourself.

Going through this self-assessment will help you understand why you feel so stuck every day, which is incredibly liberating. Team leaders often build up an identity of being the one who gets things done, and when we can't make progress, we often take it as a personal failing. We tend to brush our stress and overwhelm under the rug and just keep pushing the boulder uphill. When you start unpacking the elements of agency, it's a huge relief to realize that life at work doesn't have to be so hard—there *is* something you can do about it.

## Developing Team Agency

Reflecting on your own agency as a team leader also leads to another important realization: you are the mini CEO of your team. At least, your team members see you that way. If you're acting in a low-agency manner—tired, lacking conviction, lacking commitment, blaming others, not thinking things through—that energy is contagious. In short, your own lack of agency actively hurts your team.

When that kind of energy is the norm, no amount of bonuses, vacation days, or other incentives will counteract it. There's no point in blaming anyone or anything else, either. You can have as many "good" reasons as you want for feeling that way; none of them will stop your body language and tone from having an impact on others.

For your people, you're their CEO, whether you like it or not. There's no excuse, no passing the buck… and if you choose to remain in a victim mindset, you'll never get anywhere. Once you internalize that, you'll begin to take your own agency journey a lot more seriously.

You'll also start taking personal responsibility for developing your team's agency. Again, this follows the same process I laid out for CEOs: measure each team member on the Thrive Index and have one-on-one conversations to help them discover ways to strengthen their sense of agency. Obviously, you can't just do this once and call the job done. You'll need to follow up regularly with each person to help them continue making incremental progress. This has the added benefit of creating a feedback loop on how well you're doing at nurturing agency.

You can also open up the conversation beyond the one-on-one to the whole team. By having regular conversations in small groups about agency, you make space and time where people can learn from each other. Make it a ritual, maybe once a month, where you facilitate the conversation and create an opportunity for peer collaboration.

It's worth pointing out that sometimes, these conversations go to places where they really don't have any authority. For example, a few years ago, someone who worked for me lost some benefits from her spouse's job that had been paying for their children's schooling. Suddenly, she had to worry about where her kids would go to school, and it impacted her energy, mental focus, and well-being. There was nothing I could do about that.

Team leaders can sometimes feel extremely guilty about not being able to help. This is especially true in Asian cultures, where team leaders often take a parenting-like view of their role. They think that if they're having this open and trusting conversation with their team members, they have to solve everything.

But your team members are not children. You can care about them without solving all their problems for them. Doing that would just stifle their agency anyway. Help them help themselves, and be honest about what you can do and what you can't. Remember, Rule #1 is to bring your own motivation—you can't do that for them.

## Prioritizing Agency

For many team leaders and executives, there's one huge barrier that cuts off conversations about agency: fear of losing top performers. Let's say you have a financial analyst on your team who does fantastic work, but you suspect her real passion lies in the stock trading she does on the side, or maybe with the big data research happening in a different department. If you start talking about agency, it will lead to a conversation about her purpose and vision, and she might decide she wants to leave your team.

Prioritizing agency means being willing to let that happen. It means cultivating other people's agency is more important than serving your own short-term interests. This is absolutely essential for building a true, enduring culture of agency. Hoarding talent for your own objectives is a sure-fire way to undermine that culture and stifle agency on your team.

On the flipside, there are huge benefits to talking openly with your team members about what they genuinely want to do and achieve. They will see that you're actually on their side and breathe a sigh of relief; they no longer have to shut off a part of themselves at work. When talking about agency becomes truly acceptable, it will become the norm among the team.

That's where social agency kicks in. Your team members will start to get interested in and excited about each other's agency, and the level of rapport and cohesion will skyrocket. It goes beyond collaboration; this is how you get a team where everyone has each other's backs. Think for a second—whose back do you actually have in life? People you truly know, value, and respect. You can't mandate that. But if you commit to prioritizing agency and talking about it openly, that's what you'll get.

## Conclusion

Team leaders usually get a great start on their journey to agency. The initial training is easy, as you can see from this book. You'll probably have no trouble interpreting the ten rules and talking about them with your team.

Then come the bumps in the road. A project goes poorly, a key team member leaves, or there's a significant performance issue. Your own biases about who is a good performer and who is not start to cloud your vision. Something upsetting happens, and you fall back into your old negative emotional patterns.

For example, I recently worked with a team where regulators suddenly came in and found the company guilty of some infraction related to an incident that happened 6 years ago. The people who were responsible for that incident are gone, and the people who are there now have to deal with the fallout. Customers and clients have been asking all kinds of questions, and confidence has been shaken all around.

Those are the moments when you'll need some support to get yourself and your team back on track. When you're dealing with everyone's emotions and insecurities (including your own), as well as the business challenges, it's extremely difficult to stay focused on maintaining high agency. You need a coach, and that's where the HR leaders can help.

# 16 | For HR Leaders

A long with the CEO and team leaders, HR leaders play a crucial role in spreading agency across an organization. While CEOs set the priority and lead by example, and team leaders directly cultivate agency in their employees, HR leaders provide the training and coaching to support all these efforts. They also help adjust corporate policies, performance expectations, and incentive programs to align around agency.

This may seem simple, but it actually requires a significant shifting in mindset on the part of HR—which is a good thing. The concept of agency creates a golden opportunity for HR to achieve both better business outcomes and better human outcomes at a single stroke.

> The concept of agency creates a golden opportunity for HR to achieve both better business outcomes and better human outcomes at a single stroke.

## Rethink the Role of HR

HR has a curious relationship with the concept of agency. To understand it, we have to go back to the origins of HR in the Industrial Revolution. The concept grew out of the struggle of unions to protect worker health and well-being; the purpose of HR was to be the employee advocate, which was a confrontational role with the business leadership.

In the late twentieth century, this role shifted dramatically. With new government labor policies, and with the transition from industrial work to knowledge work, the need to protect workers was less urgent. At the same time, business leaders began trying to involve employees in the success of the business with rewards like stock options and bonuses. This is when HR started to become a partner to the business instead of an adversary. While it retained some aspects of the employee advocate role, the main focus shifted to maximizing employee productivity.

This created a bit of an identity crisis. The people who were once the champions of the common man were now often depicted in pop culture as the crony that did the management's dirty work. They were the bad guys who ruthlessly laid off thousands of people or slashed wages at a stroke. Over the next couple of decades, this "business partner" role became deeply embedded in the HR psyche.

Then around 2010, the idea of diversity, inclusion, and equity moved front and center, and the pendulum started to swing back. Once again, advocating for employees was an important part of HR's purpose. Now when I talk to senior HR professionals, I find that the dual role they play is starker than ever before. They're still strong agents of the business, doing the difficult work of executing restructures and layoffs. However, they're also doing the best they can to regain their place as allies of the employee.

The concept of agency challenges the idea that these roles are contradictory. It suggests that these two things—performance, productivity, and results on one hand and engagement, enjoyment, and fulfillment on the other—are not opposing forces. Maybe they can live together side by side. Maybe they can actually reinforce each other.

If that's true, the philosophical underpinning of HR has to change. There are no longer two separate and competing purposes; by maximizing employee agency, we can serve *both* purposes simultaneously.

This is a massive mental shift, and it won't be easy to make. There are many decades of work invested in the economic and sociological theory that capitalism is always an agent of exploitation, and management will always be at odds with labor. Most HR leaders have been steeped in this philosophy. There are still places in the world where exploitation is the norm, and even where labor policies limit the most egregious offenses, there are still many instances of people being treated terribly at work. We're not going to erase all that at a stroke.

However, we can make a start. We can focus on developing agency at the level of small teams and see how it improves both business performance and employee well-being. Then, the question for HR becomes: how far can we scale this? If agency makes a massive difference for ten employees, imagine what it could do for a hundred, a thousand, or even ten thousand or more.

This is the first step for HR leaders: to decide what you're here to do. Do you want to be a business partner and do the dirty work of management? Do you want to be an employee advocate and fight management? Or do you want to be the force that brings these two sides together in a way that's synergistic and beneficial to all?

## Raise Awareness of Agency

A crucial part of HR's job in spreading agency is to help everyone in the organization become aware of it and understand its value. One of the most powerful tools for this is data. It's one thing to think about agency philosophically; it's another to measure its impact. The key is to combine data on how people are feeling (using the Thrive Index) and how the business is doing. Those two elements need to come together at a granular level, team by team, office by office, department by department.

Do this over time—6 to 12 months at least—and a clear picture will begin to emerge of the virtuous cycle of agency. This is how you get management and shareholders to buy into this concept. The data will show that it creates value for everyone, not just one side or the other.

That's the consciousness HR has to generate. Otherwise, it would be incredibly difficult to break down the decades of capitalist-versus-socialist belief systems. Management will revert to the narrative that people are fundamentally lazy and if you don't exert discipline from the outside, they will slack off. Employees will revert to the narrative that companies only care about profits, not human beings, and work is just a means to earn a living, so there's no point in doing more than the bare minimum.

The job of HR is to not let these narratives win. It's a hard job, but it's both possible and highly rewarding. Once people start to see the virtuous cycle, it will gain momentum and become self-perpetuating. All it takes is the right combination of data and storytelling.

## Train Team Leaders

Every team leader needs to be trained in agency. This goes beyond simply teaching the ten rules; they also need to learn how to cultivate agency in their team members. How do they talk to their team members to uncover who they really are? How do they unpack and address their issues around agency? What do they do about team members who aren't making progress? All of those skills need to be trained, and it's HR's role to create the playbook and teach team leaders how to use it.

One question I often get is whether team leaders are really trainable in these skills. It's a legitimate concern; good technical people often get promoted into team leader roles but have no interest in managing people. With any given team leader, one of three things will likely happen.

One group—those who are genuinely interested in leading people—will take to this like fish to water. They'll be thrilled to finally have a playbook that helps them excel in their role the way they've always wanted. When they see the way agency helps their team members thrive, they'll become even more invested in mastering this skill.

A second group—the reluctant leaders—will find agency much more appealing than the traditional approach because it allows them to do less managing. They'll spend far less time being the disciplinarian and conflict mediator (which is what most of them really dislike about being a team leader), and more time actually solving problems (which is what they love). With a team that's self-driven and requires far less negative intervention, they might actually come to enjoy being a leader.

There will probably be a third group of people who say this is all nonsense. They'll insist that it won't work and will just distract the team from creating real value. These are usually the people who believe that human beings are fundamentally lazy, and given any sort of freedom, they will find a way to undermine the efforts of the organization or go off in the wrong direction. Probably nothing anyone says will convince these people otherwise, and because of that, they really don't belong in a leadership position at all.

As an HR leader, find out who is in each of these three camps. Don't try to guess in advance. Start teaching the idea of agency and see how the team leaders respond; it will show you who is right for the role and who is not.

## Align Policies and Practices

Although the ten rules of agency are designed to be usable in any context, some work environments make it easier than others. If your organization is truly committed to maximizing agency across the board, it may help to make some adjustments to the organization's policies and practices. The following five changes are fairly straightforward, reasonable, and non-disruptive ways to support high-agency among your employees.

### (1) Move toward a marketplace of skills.

If you remember from Chapter 2, a marketplace of skills is a workforce model where people are matched with projects and opportunities based on their entire skill set. This contrasts with the traditional model, where employees are typically on a predetermined track according to their professional degree. Some companies are already using a marketplace of skills, but many have yet to move in that direction.

This model encourages agency in multiple ways. It provides opportunities for people to take initiative—to raise their hands and say, "I want to work on that project." It makes it easier to explore different areas of the company and build a unique skill stack. It also opens the path to accelerated career growth for the superstars in your organization, which helps prevent you from losing them to your competitors. Plus, it allows people to exercise their talents more fully, which helps them simultaneously create more value *and* feel more engaged at work.

## (2) Require regular conversations about goals and career paths.

In the traditional work model, employees typically talk to their team leaders about their performance and goals no more than once or twice a year. The conversation doesn't usually go very deep; it rarely touches on personal well-being or aspirations and how they relate to work. So, it's no surprise that these perfunctory discussions do little to support the development of high agency.

However, as we established in Chapter 15, team leaders can play a huge role in cultivating their employees' agency. To do that, they need to have these one-on-one conversations much more often—not once a year but once a month, and at a much deeper level. HR has the power to shape the structure and expectations around those discussions through the systems they use to track them.

## (3) Align incentives and compensation to support agency.

As we discussed at the very beginning of this book, intrinsic motivation is typically far more powerful and sustainable than extrinsic motivation. It wouldn't make much sense to try to incentivize agency with external rewards like bonuses; the whole point is that agency is driven from within. However, it is worthwhile to make sure you're not accidentally *disincentivizing* behaviors that help people increase their agency. For example, an employee might be interested in taking on a role in a different function to help build their skill stack... but it would come with a significant pay cut. When the incentive system is actually undermining the organization's goals, that's something HR has the power to change.

### (4) Allow employees to have side hustles.

Running a side hustle is one of the most powerful things a person can do for their agency, as you know from Chapter 13. However, many companies have policies or attitudes that discourage and even prohibit this. As an HR leader, you can revisit these.

Obviously, it makes sense to disallow employees from engaging in business activities that are in direct competition with the company. However, it's counterproductive to prohibit *all* side businesses on the assumption that they distract employees from their main jobs. This places unnecessary limitations on employees' personal freedom and prevents them from doing things that would be beneficial to their well-being *and* their productivity—things like learning new skills, growing their network, feeding their sense of purpose, and centering their perspective.

## Provide Agency Coaching

As we discussed in Chapter 15, training people in the concept and practice of agency is not particularly difficult. The bigger challenge is to keep them on track over the long term, especially when work and life throw them curve balls. That's going to require a cadre of coaches whose only job is to help employees advance their own agency.

It's not unlike the psychologist in the television drama *Billions*. The show is centered on a hedge fund, which employs a psychologist whose role is to take care of the mental well-being of the traders. She's not there to be a safety blanket; her job is to keep them sharp, hungry, competitive. That's an important function modern organizations will have to play: investing dedicated resources to build strong levels of agency in the workforce.

The reality is, although the concept of agency may be easy to understand, it's not an easy habit to build. People do not learn how to take initiative and ownership when they're kids in school; they learn to follow instructions. For most people, that's still their default habit. Breaking that habit and replacing it with a new one takes deliberate, repeated effort over time. It's like gardening—without periodic attention, the weeds will grow and take over. People will fall back into their old ways and beliefs.

> It's like gardening—without periodic attention, the weeds will grow and take over. People will fall back into their old ways and beliefs.

How many coaches are we talking about? You'll probably need one coach for every 20 or 30 teams. So, for an organization with 10,000 people and around 500–600 teams, we're talking about 20 to 25 coaches. This may sound like a big cost, but it's miniscule compared to the financial gains that result from cultivating agency. First of all, organizations currently spend significant resources planning career paths for their employees; that becomes largely unnecessary in a high-agency organization where employees build their own career paths. More importantly, higher agency leads to higher productivity, lower turnover, and more creative problem-solving. Honestly, it's hard to beat the ROI on this investment.

## Conclusion

From my conversations with HR professionals, it's clear that most HR people would love to do this. Deep down, they know they came into this profession to do more than fight with management for a $2 raise for everyone, or to decide who stays and who goes in the next restructuring. They genuinely believe these two narratives can come together, but until now they didn't know how to do it. Agency is what makes it possible.

# Final Thoughts

L ast year, something fascinating happened with my team. In January, the leadership team came together to discuss the overall market for consulting. The industry in general is going through a bit of turmoil, with many recent CEO turnovers among the companies who make up our client base. In those boardrooms, people are more interested in going back to basics than doing large, creative transformations. We decided to pivot our solutions to support that.

Normally, we would set up internal task forces to run a top-down strategic review. Instead, I put my thesis around agency to the test and asked small teams of practitioners to develop a blueprint for moving forward. I insisted that the leadership team *not* direct the action, only provide support when asked. Throughout the whole process, I was tapped for input only two or three times, and the same was true for others on the leadership team. When it came time for the teams to present their results, I had very little idea what to expect.

They *blew me away*. The depth, clarity, passion, and focus was beyond my wildest dreams. Even if the leadership team had done the work ourselves, we probably wouldn't have produced anything quite as sharp.

Afterward, I asked another partner what she had learned that day. She said the one thing that impressed her above all else was that none of the teams had asked for permission. They had simply presented their hypotheses, their logic, their evidence, and their proposed solutions. They had taken full ownership over the problem and brought all their capabilities to bear on it.

It was a powerful validation of the agency concept to see young people step up in this way in the middle of one of the busiest seasons of our work. I would have expected them to try to outdo each other, but instead, the teams coordinated behind the scenes, all without any kind of project management structure on top. Take a moment to fully appreciate this: we got a prioritized, integrated, coordinated plan of action *without any project managers*. The most senior people involved were a couple of senior consultants with 5 or 6 years of experience apiece.

It's astonishing what can be achieved when a group of high-agency people comes together.

I went to business school in 1996, and around that time, there was a significant shift in the way CEOs were thinking about productivity in organizations. Major shifts were already underway in the world of work, and leaders were starting to feel the effects. Their time-test management practices were starting to crack under the strain of change.

Until that point, the primary management lens was "performance." Every company wanted to create an environment where high performance would happen every day. In practice, this manifested as the standard Jack Welch playbook: set the company strategy; choose specific, measurable goals; cascade those goals to KPIs for each person; and tie management and compensation to those KPIs.

What we forgot in implementing this playbook is our *humanity*. We weren't paying attention to how human motivation and creativity actually worked. In driving those KPIs, we were imposing goals on people from the outside. They were working in service of someone else's dreams and aspirations. And their attention became so focused on those specific targets that they became siloed from everything else happening around them.

Instead of driving human performance ever higher, we were inadvertently putting a *ceiling* on it. That's why, if you look at the management research over the last 30 years, you will rarely come across organizations where employees routinely outperform their KPIs. The vast majority consistently underperform, and in retrospect, that makes sense. When someone else tells you how high to jump and constantly monitors you, they've taken away your creative energy and intrinsic motivation to jump any higher than that… even though the capability to do so is within you.

The most transformational organizations of the last 30 years—companies like Google, Meta, and Amazon—understood this early on. They began experimenting with different ways of working, like organizing themselves into small, agile teams, and intentionally dedicating time for exploratory, creative work. They were even speaking a different language about work, using terms like autonomy, "growth mindset," and "psychological safety." Those were the companies that grew at 10 times or 100 times the market rate—the ones that rejected the traditional management approach.

For many leaders, it's extremely difficult to accept that the high-performance playbook might be flawed. The management world has embraced it so fully and practiced it for so long; you'll be hard-pressed to find a CEO anywhere who doesn't want to build a high-performance culture. We're so invested in this idea that virtually no one questions it.

Why? Because it guarantees that people will jump. In that way, it's the mediocre company's best friend.

But we need to ask ourselves a brutally honest question. If change and complexity are accelerating, if today's problems require the combined creativity of many people across many disciplines, if it's becoming harder and harder to get people to jump to the heights we need, does the high-performance playbook really work anymore? Or is it time for a new management lens?

It has taken me almost 30 years to fully understand what that new lens should be. What we need isn't a high-performance workforce—it's a *high-agency workforce.*

> What we need isn't a high-performance workforce—it's a *high-agency workforce.*

That isn't to say that the high-performance playbook was a total failure. It created a lot of wealth and helped a lot of companies survive for a long time. We can give credit where credit is due and at the same time ask whether this approach is really fit for purpose in the world of modern work. We have all become so burned out... is it worth the mental illness we're creating? Is there a better way? Is it possible to be both 10 times happier *and* 10 times more productive at work? Shouldn't we at least give ourselves the chance to find out?

That's the premise of this whole journey. This new approach—the high-agency playbook—is just as simple, intuitive, and practical as the old one, but it's based on accurate principles of human motivation. If you want someone to truly fulfill their potential and do their best work, carrots and sticks will *not* suffice. As we now understand, people thrive best when they're intrinsically motivated, that's exactly what the ten rules of agency are designed for.

When I talk to leaders about agency, the one real challenge I get is this: what about the business results? The old high-performance playbook was directly linked to financial results, which was comforting. Leaders could set the targets at the top and cascade them down, so in theory, if everyone hits their KPIs, the company should get the results it aimed for. That's not the case with agency... so what if you invest in creating a high-agency workforce, but the gains don't show?

That's a fair question. The truth is, there is a time lag. From the moment you start cultivating agency to the moment it shows on the P&L, you can expect a gap of at least a few months, and you have to build that into your assumptions. This is a learning process for everyone; high agency won't happen overnight. But as long as your business relies on creative energy and collaboration, the curve of agency and the curve of results will go hand in hand, with a slight phase lag.

The real beauty of high agency is that it sustains itself. You don't have to shout at everyone every week. You don't have to ratchet up the bonuses every year. You don't have to pump people up with speeches or parties. If you are patient and persistent in cultivating the seedlings of agency, it will get to the point where it just *happens* without any external intervention at all. And because high agency is self-sustaining, so are the results it generates for the business.

> The real beauty of high agency
> is that it sustains itself.

Some people look at incumbent companies like Google and Amazon—the early rejectors of the traditional management playbook—and say they're one disruption away from becoming irrelevant. In reality, that hasn't been the case. They've been amazing at evolving on a regular basis. It's not because the water in Silicon Valley is different; it's because they've managed to build the basic principles of high agency into their workforce.

There are big challenges coming to the world of work. We're already seeing massive disruption from automation and AI, there is certainly more to come. The people and companies that find agency will also find a way to evolve and thrive.

Agency, human agency, is not an office or a structure. It is the power within oneself to be the best you can be and to uplift yourself—not being a victim and exerting that power to benefit yourself and those around you, including your work. Agency at work works if you know how to harness your own agency.

Where are you in your agency? How are you with your agency?

# References

Cappelli, Peter and Anna Tavis (2016). The Performance Management Revolution: The focus is shifting from accountability to learning. Harvard Business Review. October 2016. https://hbr.org/2016/10/the-performance-management-revolution

Confino, Paolo (2024). Could AI create a one-person unicorn? Sam Altman thinks so—and Silicon Valley sees the technology 'waiting for us'. Yahoo!Finance. February 4, 2024. https://finance.yahoo.com/news/could-ai-create-one-person-120000722.html

Cordon, Miguel (2024). OpenAI's Paris-based rival raises $640m at $6b valuation. Tech in Asia. June 12, 2024. https://www.techinasia.com/mistral-ai-raises-640m-ai-craze

Edmondson, Amy C. (2012). Teaming: How Organizations Learn, Innovate, and Compete in the Knowledge Economy. Jossey-Bass: Hoboken, NJ. 352 pages.

Gartner (2023). Gartner HR Survey Reveals Less Than Half of Employees Are Achieving Optimal Performance. May 23, 2023. https://www.gartner.com/en/newsroom/press-releases/05-23-2023-gartner-hr-survey-reveals-less-than-half-of-employees-are-achieving-optimal-performance

Hagel, John, John Seely Brown, Maggie Wooll, and Alok Ranjan (2017). If you love them, set them free. Deloitte. 06 June 2017. https://www2.deloitte.

com/content/dam/insights/us/articles/2725_if-you-love-them-set-them-free/DUP_If-you-love-them-set-them-free.pdf

Harter, Jim (2020). Thriving Employees Create a Thriving Business. Gallup. June 26, 2020. https://www.gallup.com/workplace/313067/employees-aren-thriving-business-struggling.aspx

Lowisz, Steve (2023). Leaders, Don't Be Fooled—You Can't Beat Burnout With A Yoga Mat. Forbes. July 26, 2023. https://www.forbes.com/sites/insights-adobe-microsoft/2025/03/31/your-guide-to-marketing-in-the-era-of-ai/

Microsoft (2023). Will AI Fix Work. May 9, 2023. https://www.microsoft.com/en-us/worklab/work-trend-index/will-ai-fix-work/

Pink, Daniel H. (2009). Drive: The Surprising Truth about What Motivates Us. Riverhead Books: New York. 242 pages.

Roy, Indranil, Duleesha Kulasooriya, Clarissa Turner, and Vicnan Pannirselvam (2020). Remote work: A temporary 'bug' becomes a permanent 'feature'. Deloitte. https://www2.deloitte.com/content/dam/Deloitte/sg/Documents/human-capital/sg-hc-remote-work.pdf

Stelter, Susan (2022). Want to Advance in Your Career? Build Your Own Board of Directors. Harvard Business Review. May 9, 2022. https://hbr.org/2022/05/want-to-advance-in-your-career-build-your-own-board-of-directors

The Adecco Group (2021). Burnout Might Be The New Worker Pandemic. Half Of Leaders Struggle To See The Signs. September 6, 2021. https://www.adeccogroup.com/future-of-work/latest-insights/burnout-might-be-the-new-worker-pandemic-half-of-leaders-struggle-to-see-the-signs

The Economist (2023). Pity the modern manager—burnt-out, distracted and overloaded. October 24, 2023. https://www.economist.com/business/2023/10/24/pity-the-modern-manager-burnt-out-distracted-and-overloaded

Tsatiris, Dimitrios (2022). A Simple Formula to Help Solve the Riddle of Anxiety: An equation to help reduce anxiety. Psychology Today. March 26, 2022. https://www.psychologytoday.com/us/blog/anxiety-in-high-achievers/202203/simple-formula-help-solve-the-riddle-anxiety

World Economic Forum (2025). The Future of Jobs Report 2025. 7 January 2025. https://www.weforum.org/publications/the-future-of-jobs-report-2025/

# Index

www.ingramcontent.com/pod-product-compliance
Lightning Source LLC
Chambersburg PA
CBHW061242220326
41599CB00028B/5509